The Beauties of Nature COLOURING BOOK

The Beauties
of Nature
COLOURING
BOOK

120 STUNNING PICTURES
WITH FULL COLOURING GUIDES

ARCTURUS

ARCTURUS

This edition published in 2017 by Arcturus Publishing Limited
26/27 Bickels Yard, 151–153 Bermondsey Street,
London SE1 3HA

ISBN: 978-1-78599-372-5
CH005080NT
Supplier 29, Date 0617, Print run 6414

Printed in China

Created for children aged 10+

Introduction

Images from the natural world have always fascinated people – not only experts, but also those of us who simply admire its beauty. Birds, butterflies, flowers and fish are wonderful subjects to paint and draw, but can be difficult if you are not an experienced artist. An easy way to practise your artistic skills is by colouring in, which can quickly reward you with a pleasing result. And there is no better way to learn art than by copying the work of a master.

In the days before photography, accurate, detailed paintings were the only way of providing a visual record of a species. The plates in this book are taken from a range of historical sources. The flowers are drawn from *Choix des Plus Belles Fleurs* (Choice of the Most Beautiful Flowers) by Pierre-Joseph Redouté, published in 1827. The birds are taken from two sources: *A History of the Birds of Europe* (1871) by H.E. Dresser and *The Birds of America* (1840–44) by John T. Bowen and John James Audubon. For the butterflies and fish, we turned to *The Naturalist's Library*, which was edited by the great Scottish naturalist Sir William Jardine (1800–1874). The illustrations were engraved by William Lizars (1788–1859).

The choice of art materials you can use for colouring is very wide: oil-based, wax-based or watersoluble colour pencils all give great results. You can use them dry, blending them with your fingers or a paper stump, or dilute them with oil, or water for the watersoluble pencils. Whichever medium you choose, you'll derive many hours of enjoyment from colouring these beauties of nature.

KEY: *List of plates*

1 Crown imperial – yellow

2 Firecrest

3 *Pieris epicharis*

4 *Gloxinia*

5 Waxwing

6 *Leptocircus*

7 *Amaryllis*

8 Western bluebird

9 *Papilio protesilaus*

10 *Narcissus*

11 Harris's buzzard

12 *Marius thetis*

13 Japanese camellia

14 Common redstart

15 *Polommatus venus*

16 One-spotted mesoprion

17 Tulip

18 Common kingfisher

19 *Thaliura rhipheus*

20 Common hyacinth

21 Golden oriole

22 *Argynnis adippe*

23 Poppy

24 Azure-winged magpie

25 *Polyommatus marsyas*

26 Dutch iris

27 Eagle owl

28 *Rhipheus dasycephalus*

29 Blanket flower

30 Red-rumped swallow

31 *Deiopeia bella*

32 Pink-tailed chaleus

33 Snapdragon

34 Dalmatian pelican

35 *Gonepteryx rhamni*

36 Blue false indigo

37 Black-headed bunting

38 *Helicopis gnidus*

39 Chinese peony

40 Rose-coloured starling

41 *Nymphalis ethiocles*

42 Winged-stem passion flower

43 Lazuli bunting

44 *Peridromia arethusa*

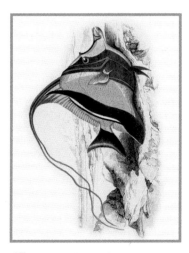

45 Horned zanclus

46 Knysna lily

47 Common redpoll

48 *Heleona fenestrata*

49 Fringed iris

50 Pine grosbeak

51 *Colias hyale*

52 Harlequin flower

53 Griffon vulture

54 *Cethosia cyane*

55 Angel's trumpet

56 Northern cardinal

57 *Heliconia erato*

58 Crown imperial

59 Greater flamingo

60 *Melitaea athalia*

61 Blue Egyptian water lily

62 Common buttonquail

63 *Papilio ascanius*

64 Hanging bells

65 Two-barred crossbill

66 *Heliconia flora*

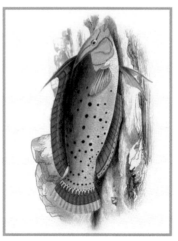

67 Radiated weaver

68 *Hippeastrum*

69 Swallow-tailed flycatcher

70 *Argynnis paphia*

71 Lady's-slipper orchid

72 Common kestrel

73 *Charaxes jasius*

74 *Auricula*

75 Northern bullfinch

76 *Limacodes micilia*

77 Tulip tree

78 American goldfinch

79 *Euploea limniace*

80 Blue plantain lily

81 Brandt's jay

82 *Hipparchia semele*

83 Sulphur rose

84 Townsend's warbler

85 *Callidryas eubule*

86 Sweet pea

87 Common starling

88 *Lycaena chryseis*

89 Dwarf morning glory

90 Long-eared owl

91 *Pieris belisama*

92 Wolf fish

93 Oleander

94 Steller's jay

95 *Saturnia cynthia*

96 Snake vine

97 Purple heron

98 *Polyommatus argiolus*

99 Heartsease

100 White-throated kingfisher

101 *Vanessa atalanta*

102 Cabbage rose

103 Hawfinch

104 *Papilio machaon*

105 Common peony

106 Green woodpecker

107 *Catochala neogama*

108 Spanish iris

109 Golden-winged warbler

110 *Urania sloanus*

111 *Lychnis coronata*

112 Red-backed shrike

113 *Polyommatus arion*

114 Golden-tailed masoprion

115 Poppy anemone

116 Double-crested cormorant

117 *Cethosia dido*

118 Dahlia

119 Common wood pigeon

120 Caterpillars

2

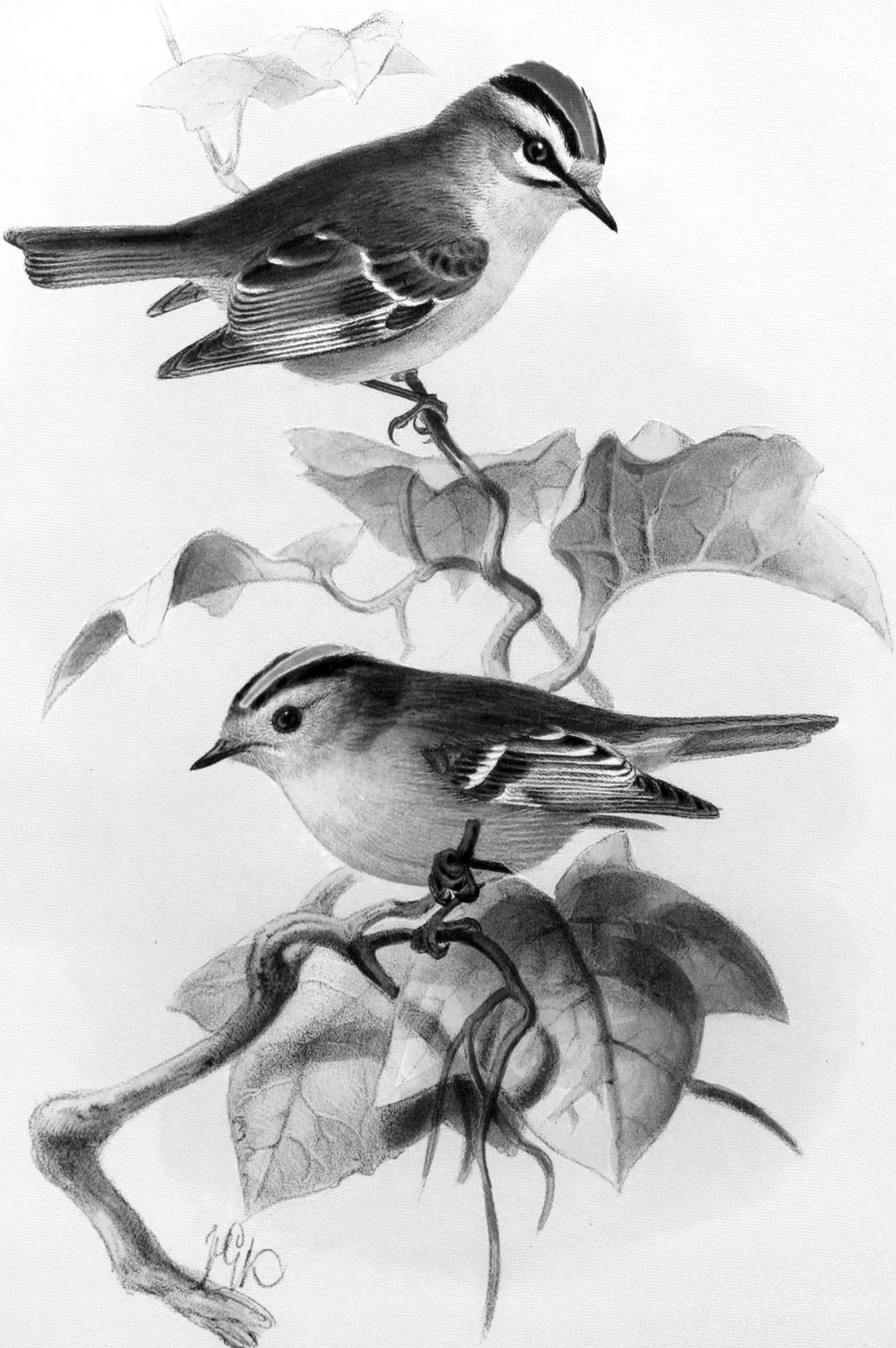

4

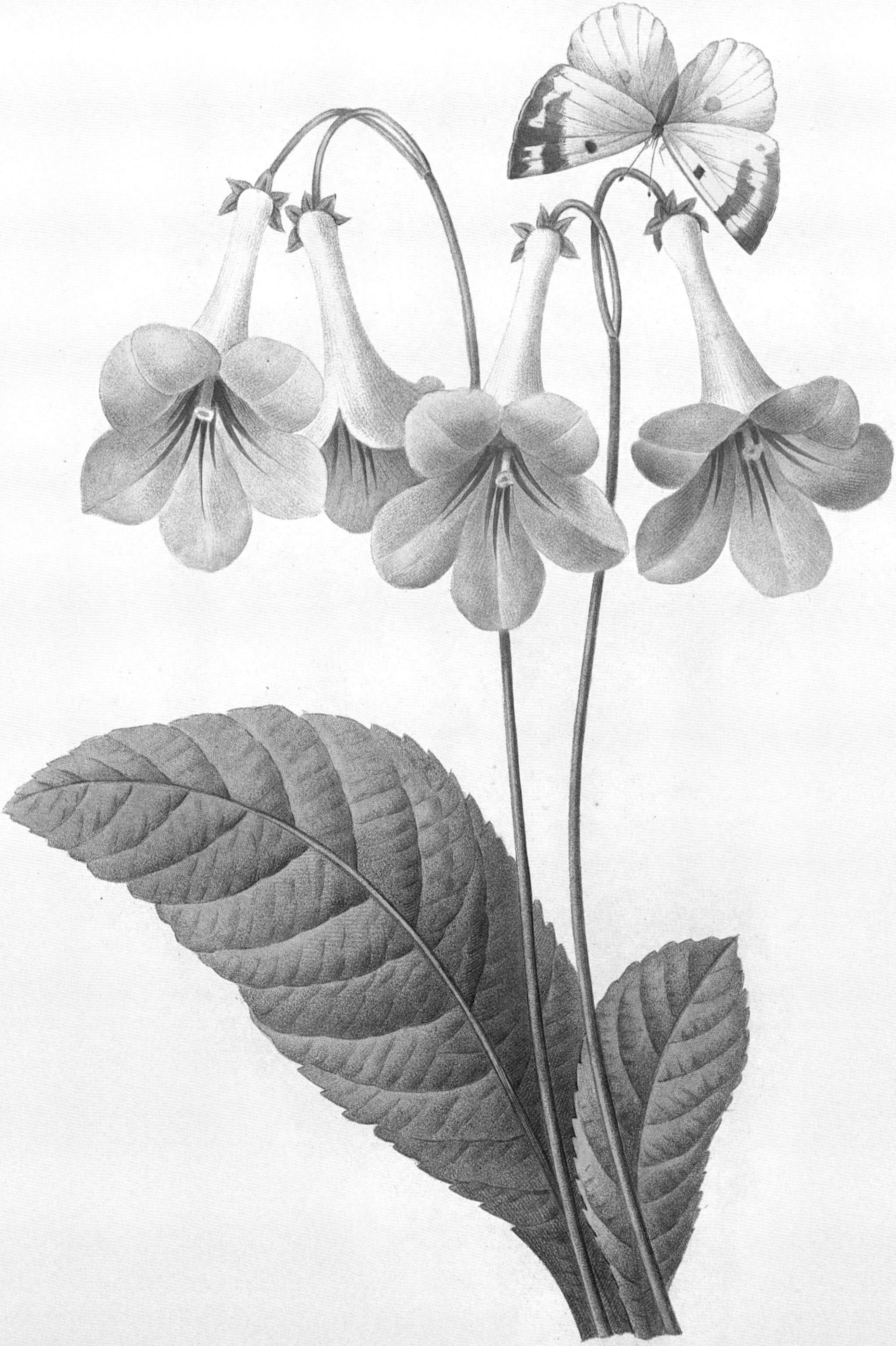

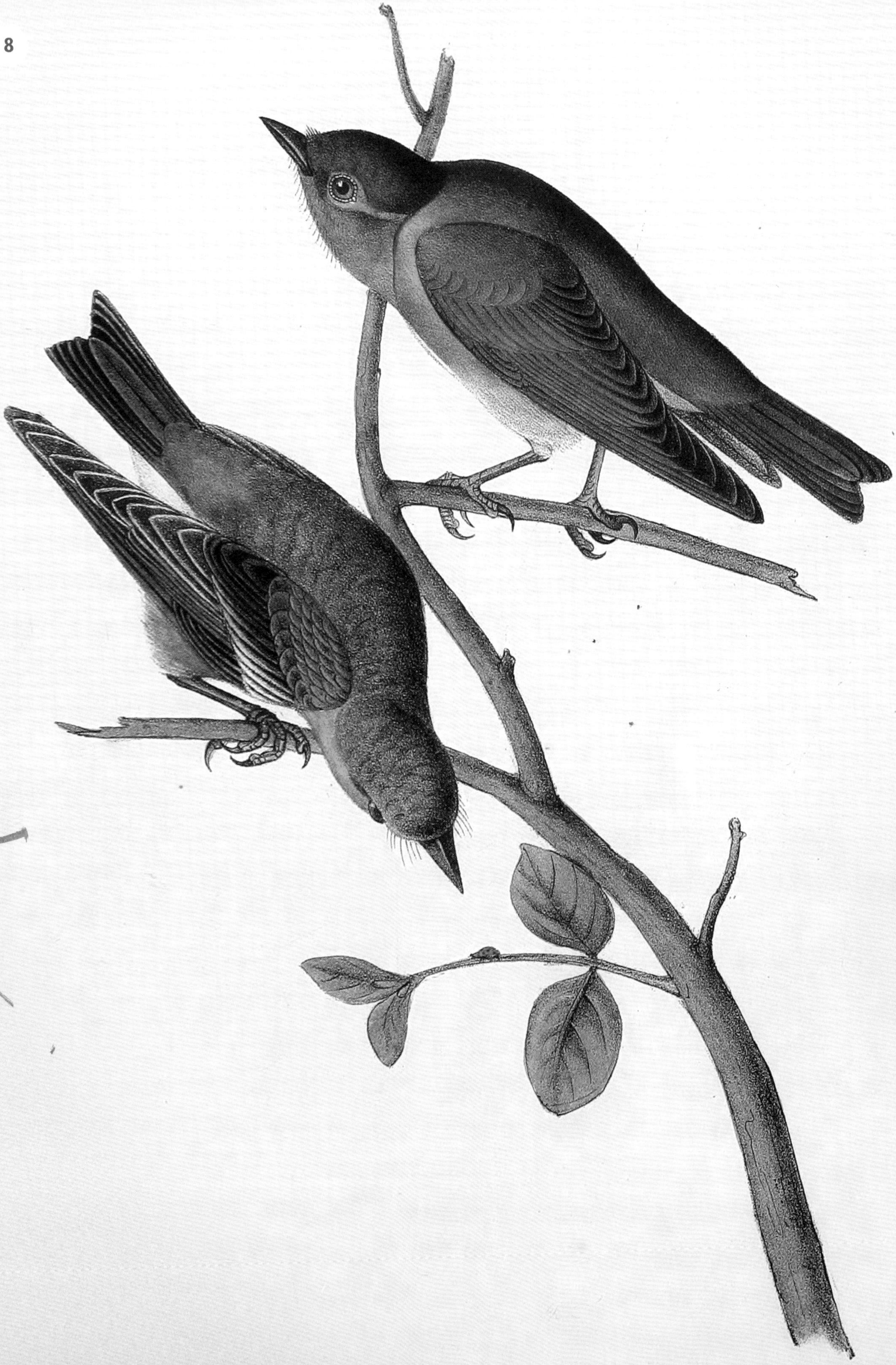

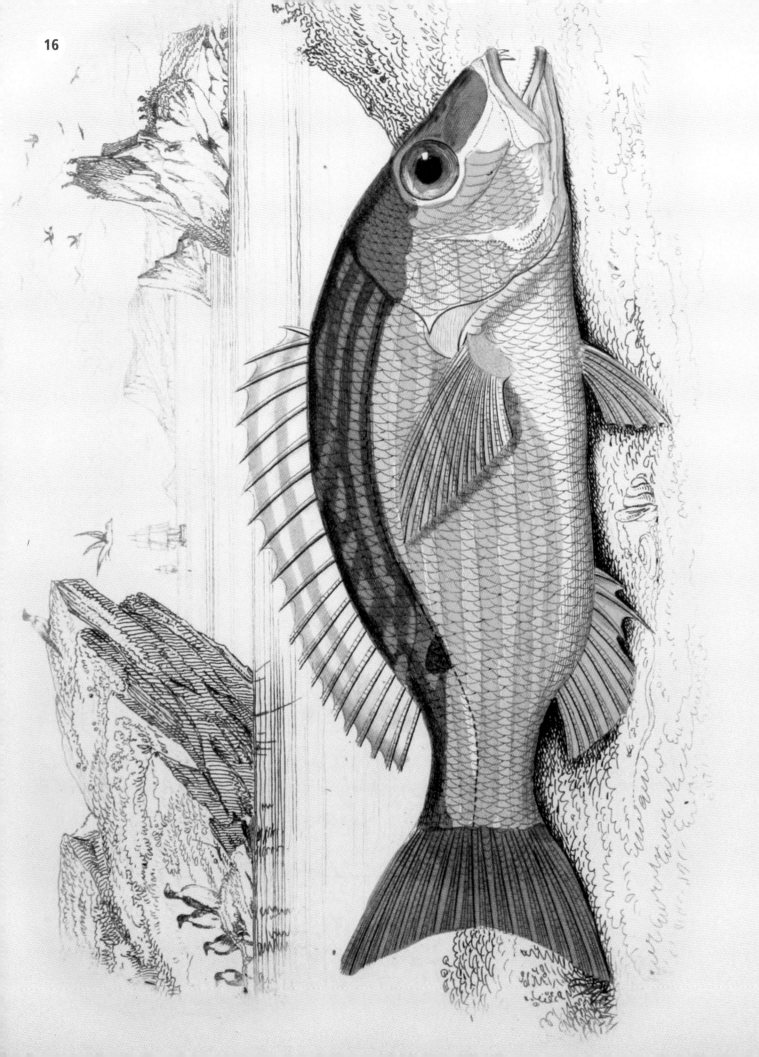

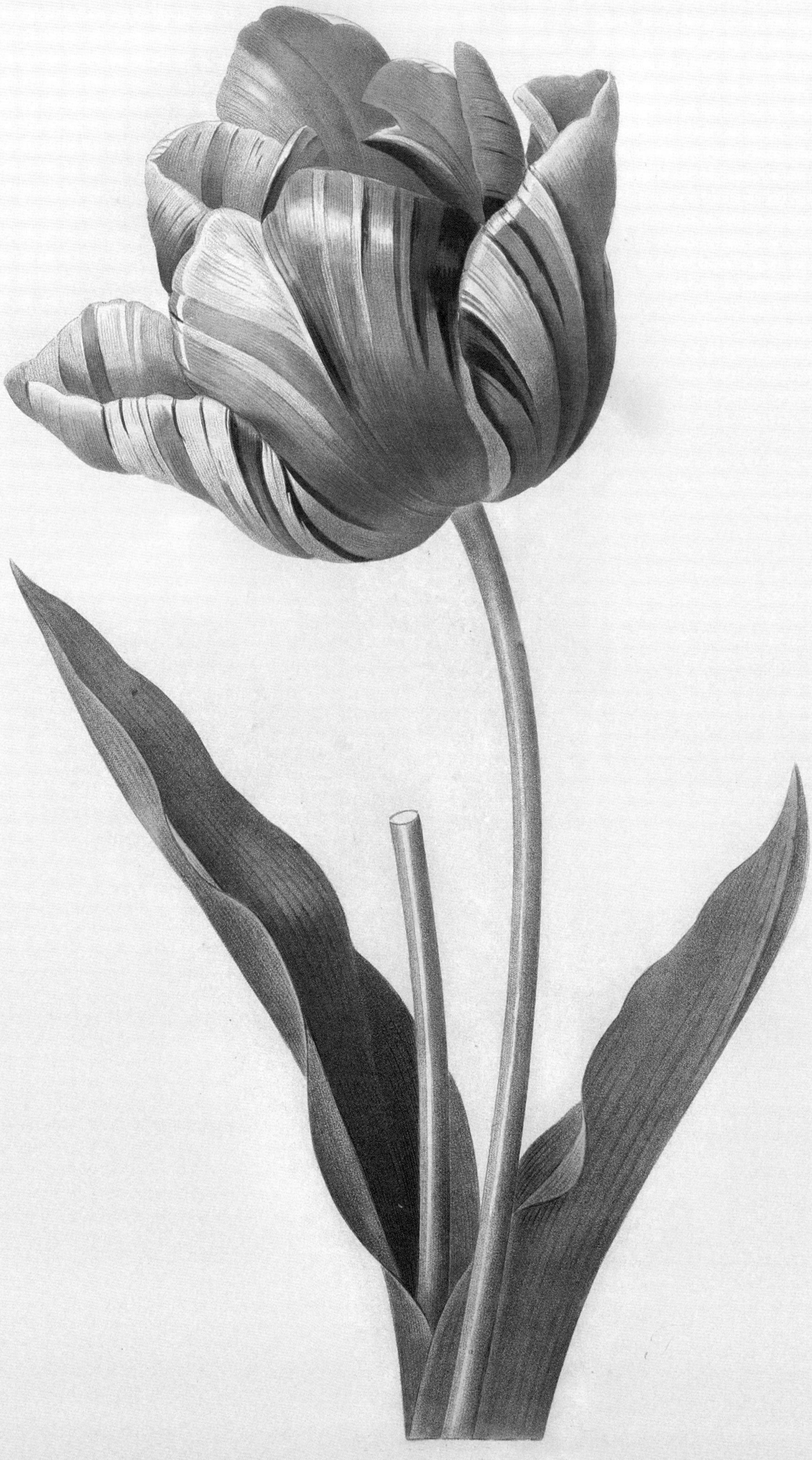

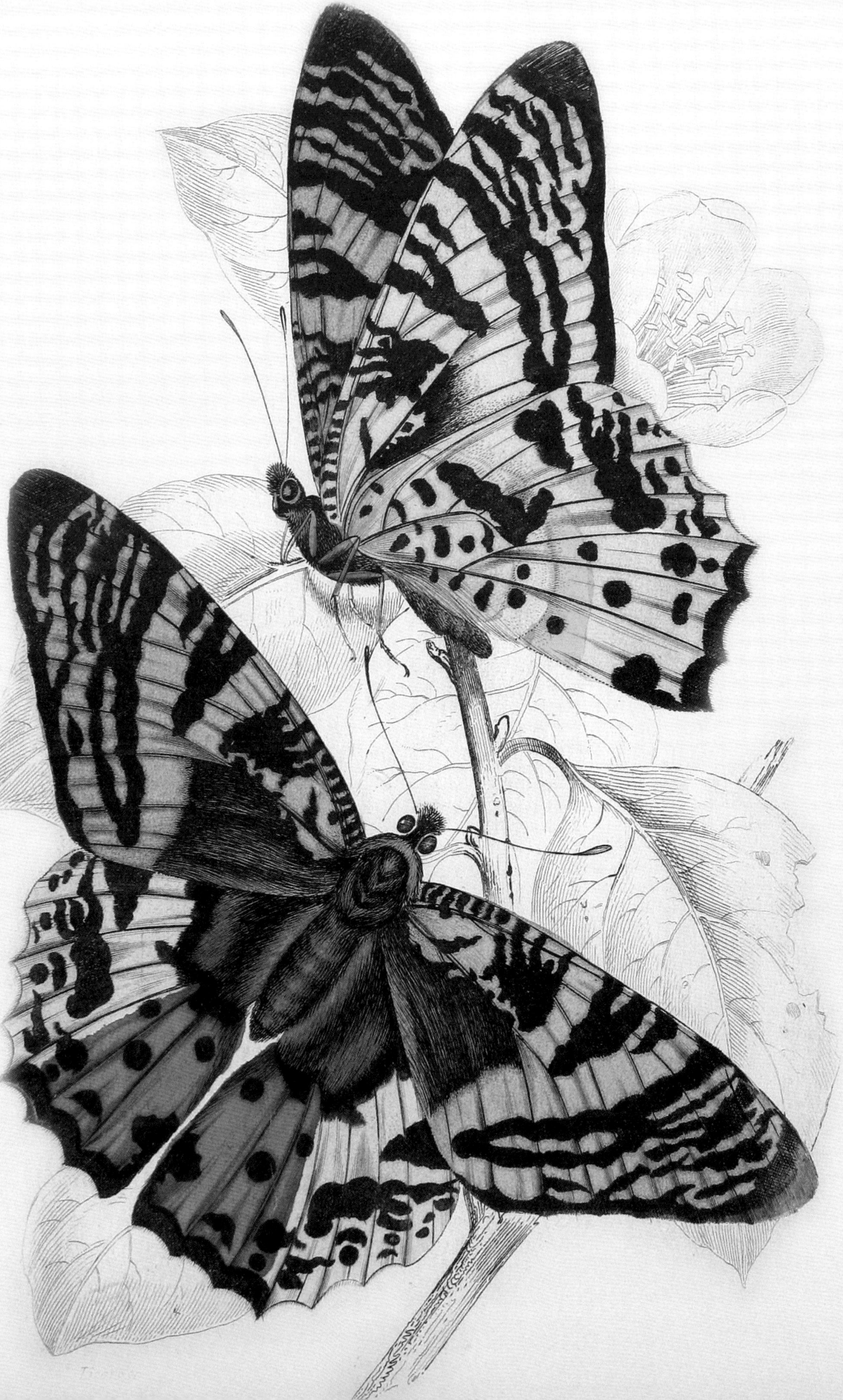

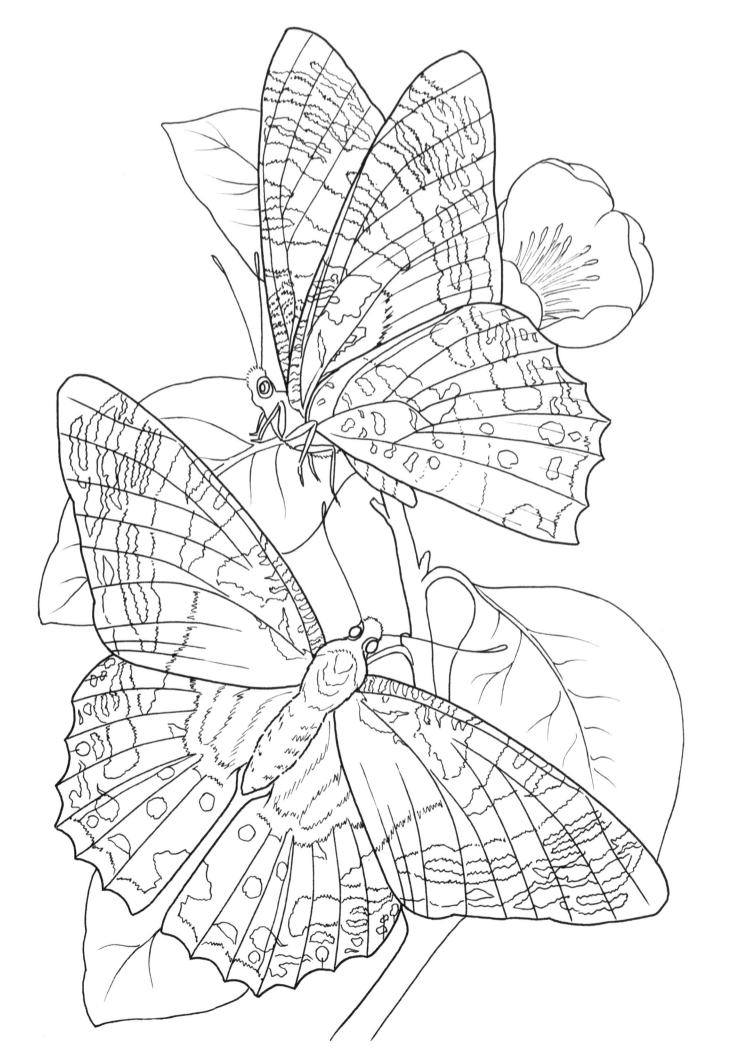

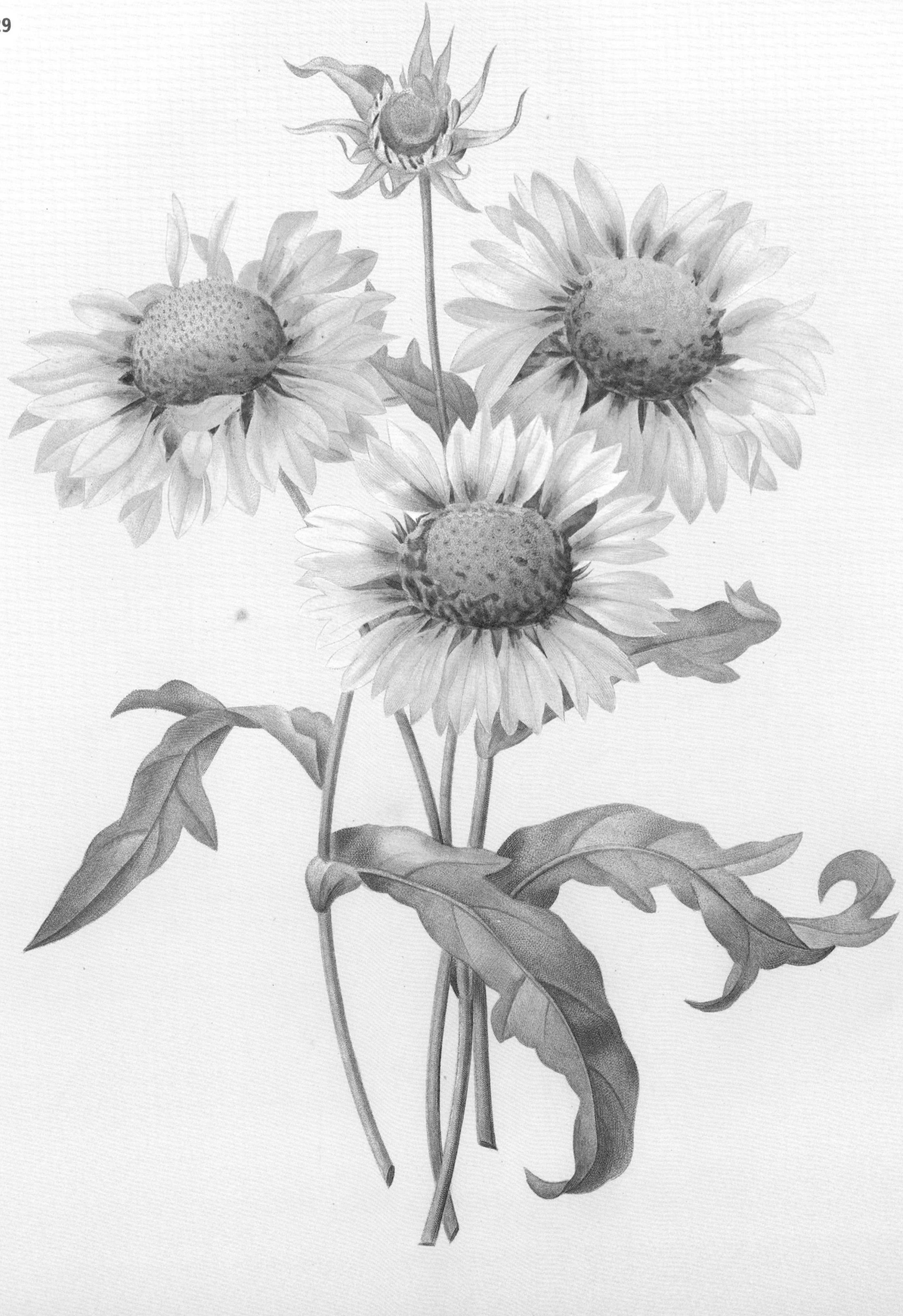

1

2

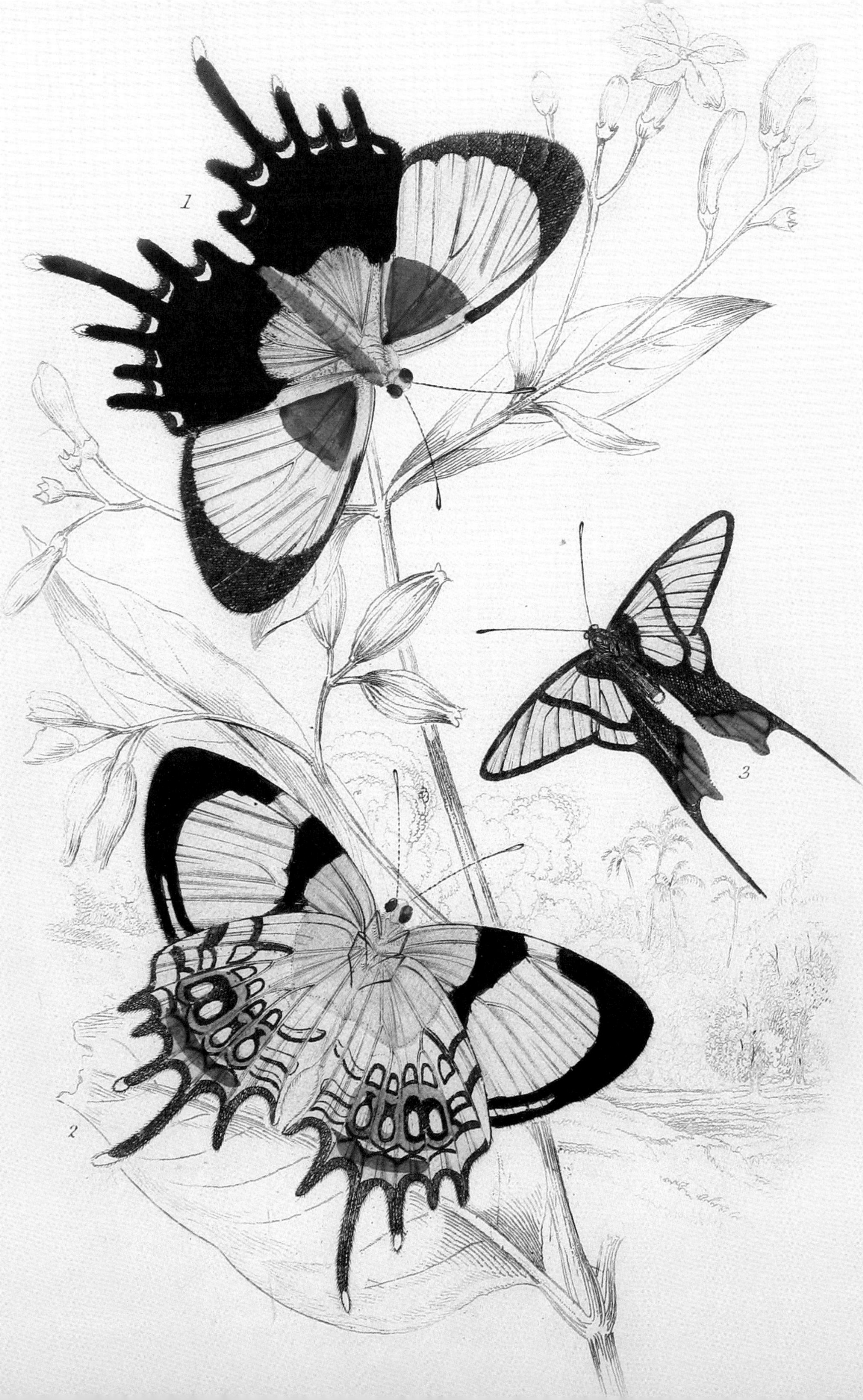
1
3
2

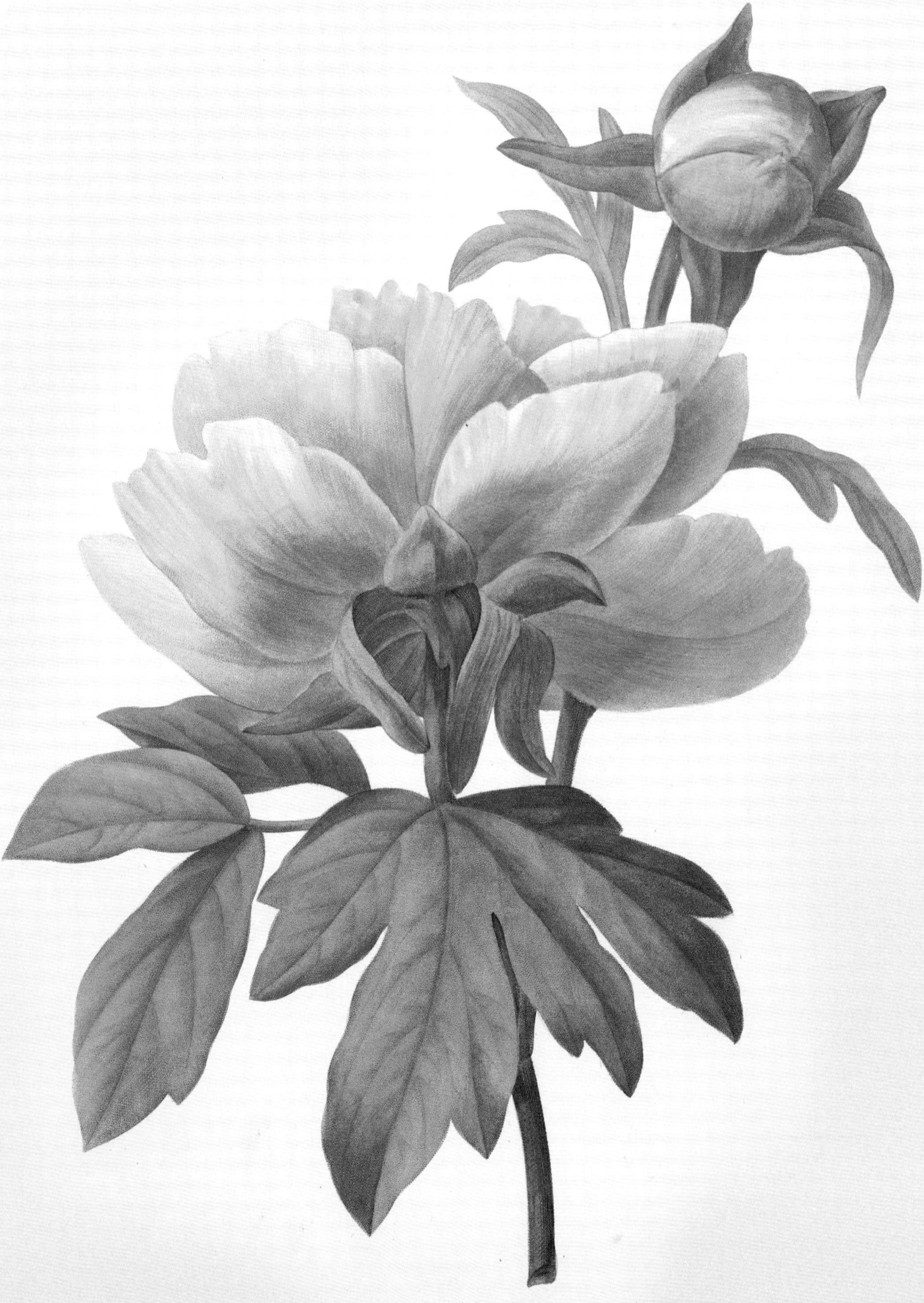

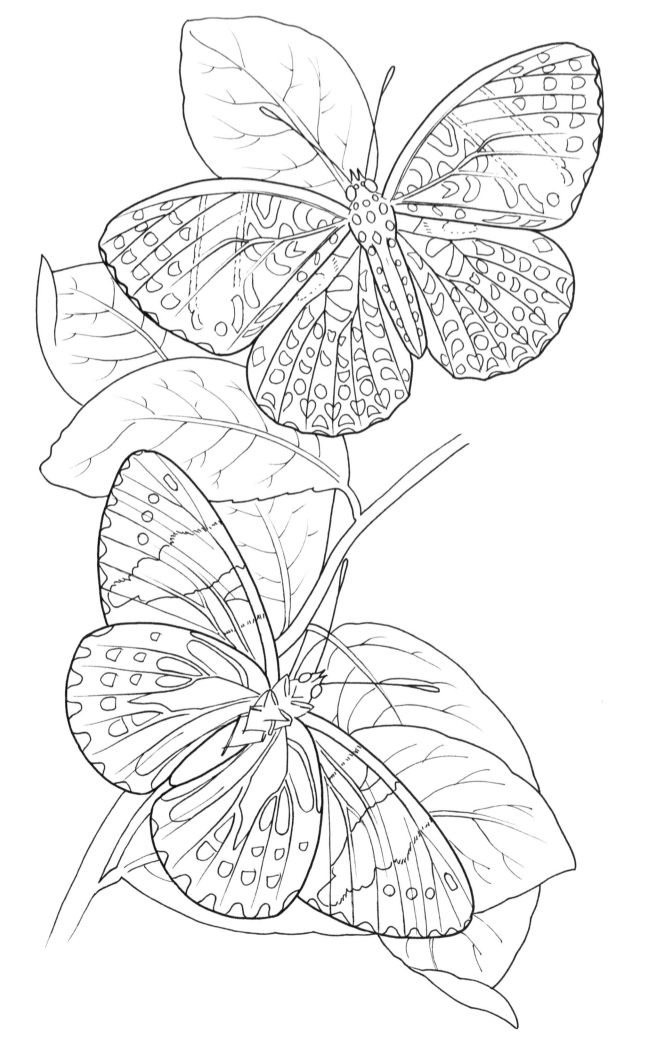

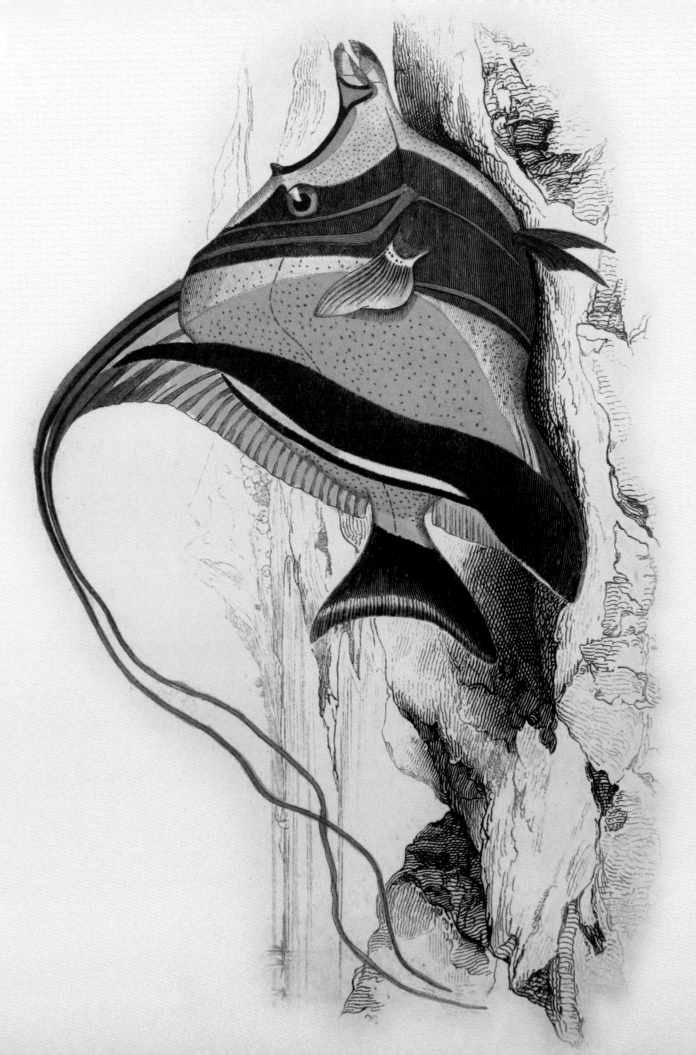

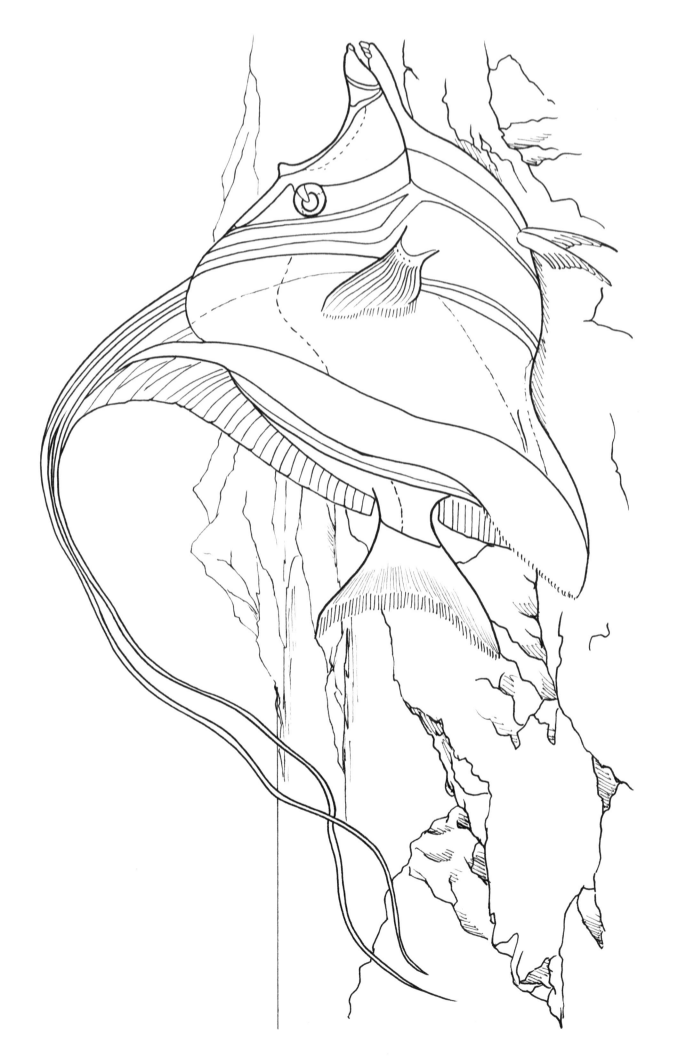

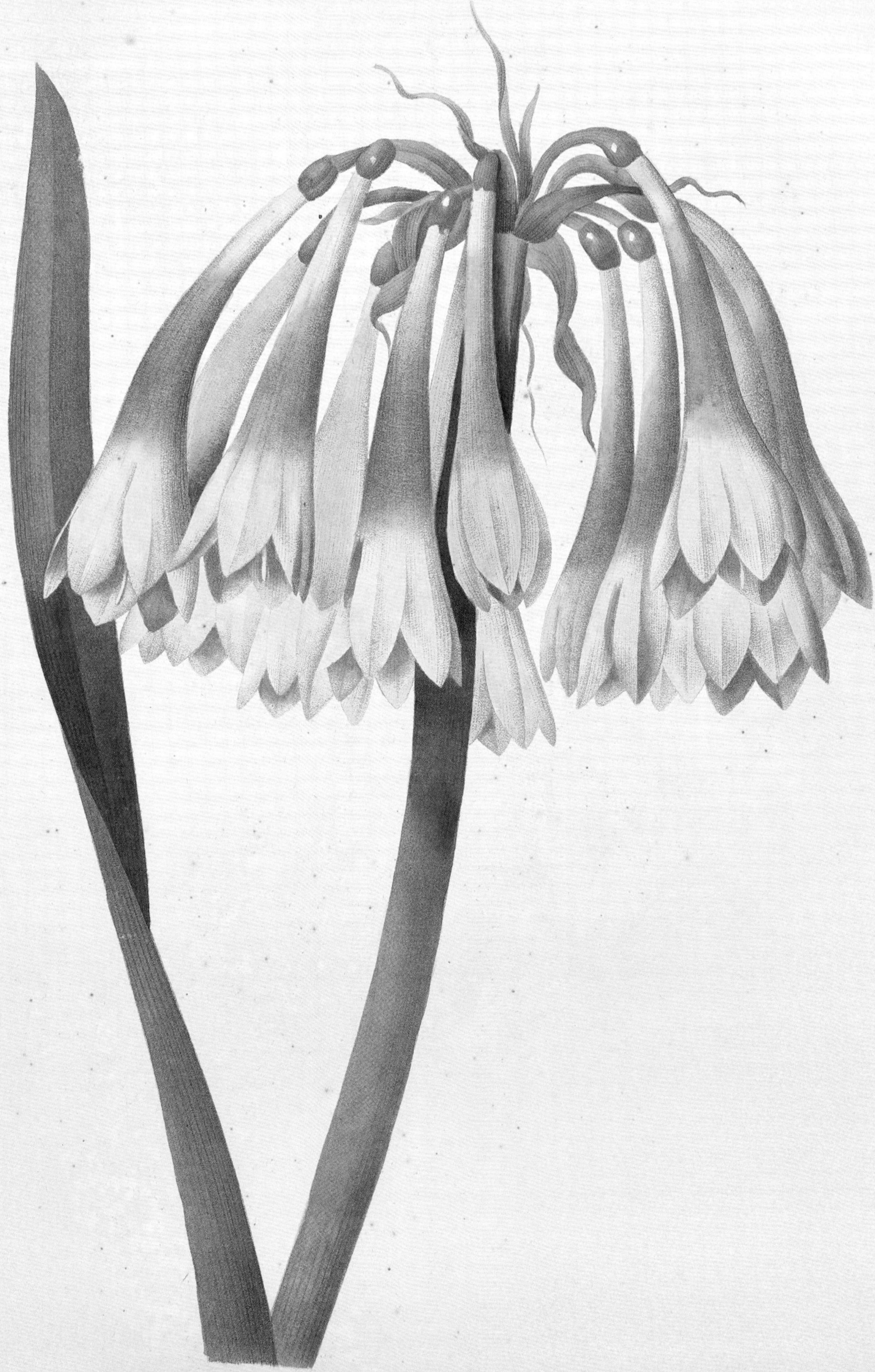

49

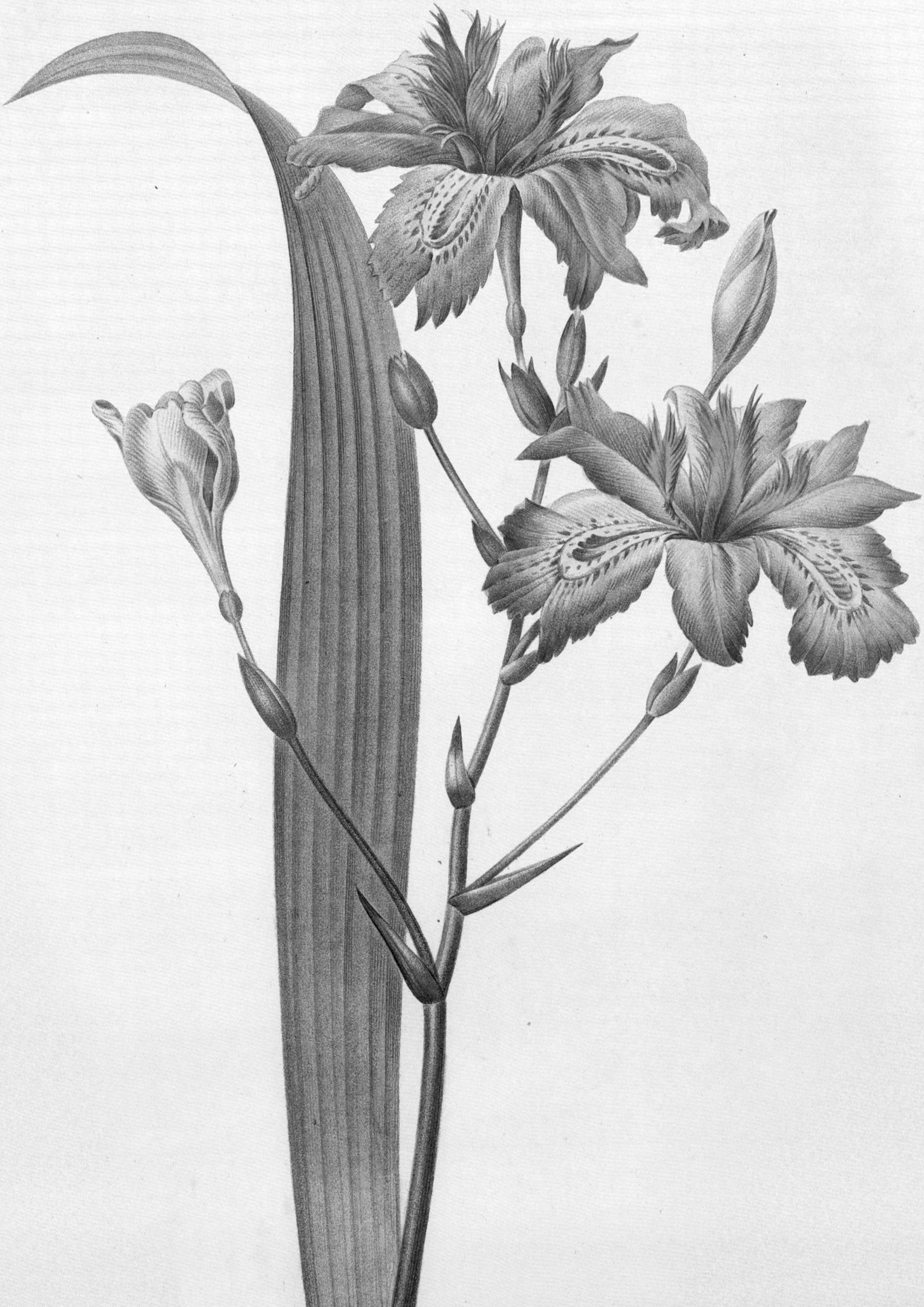

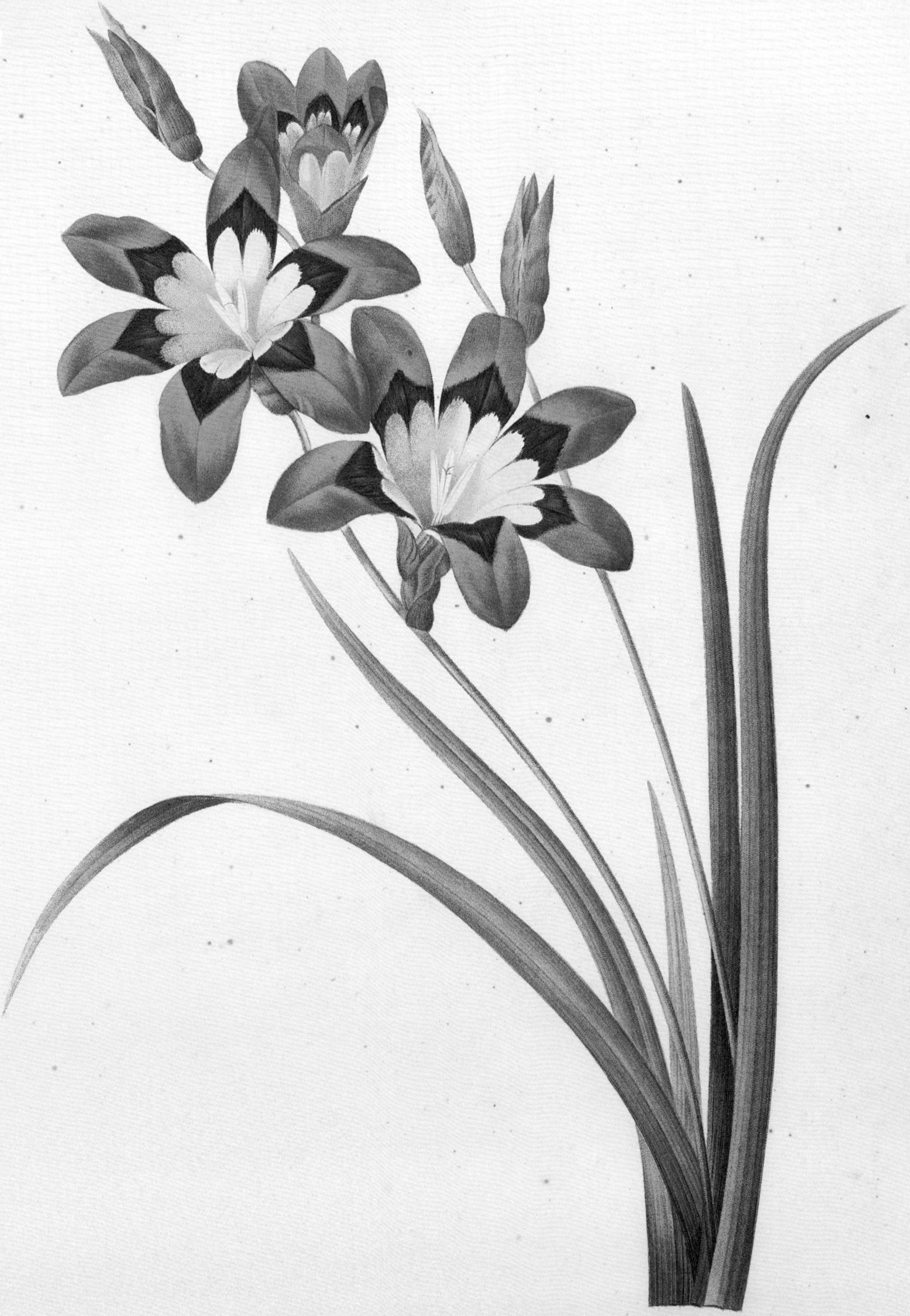

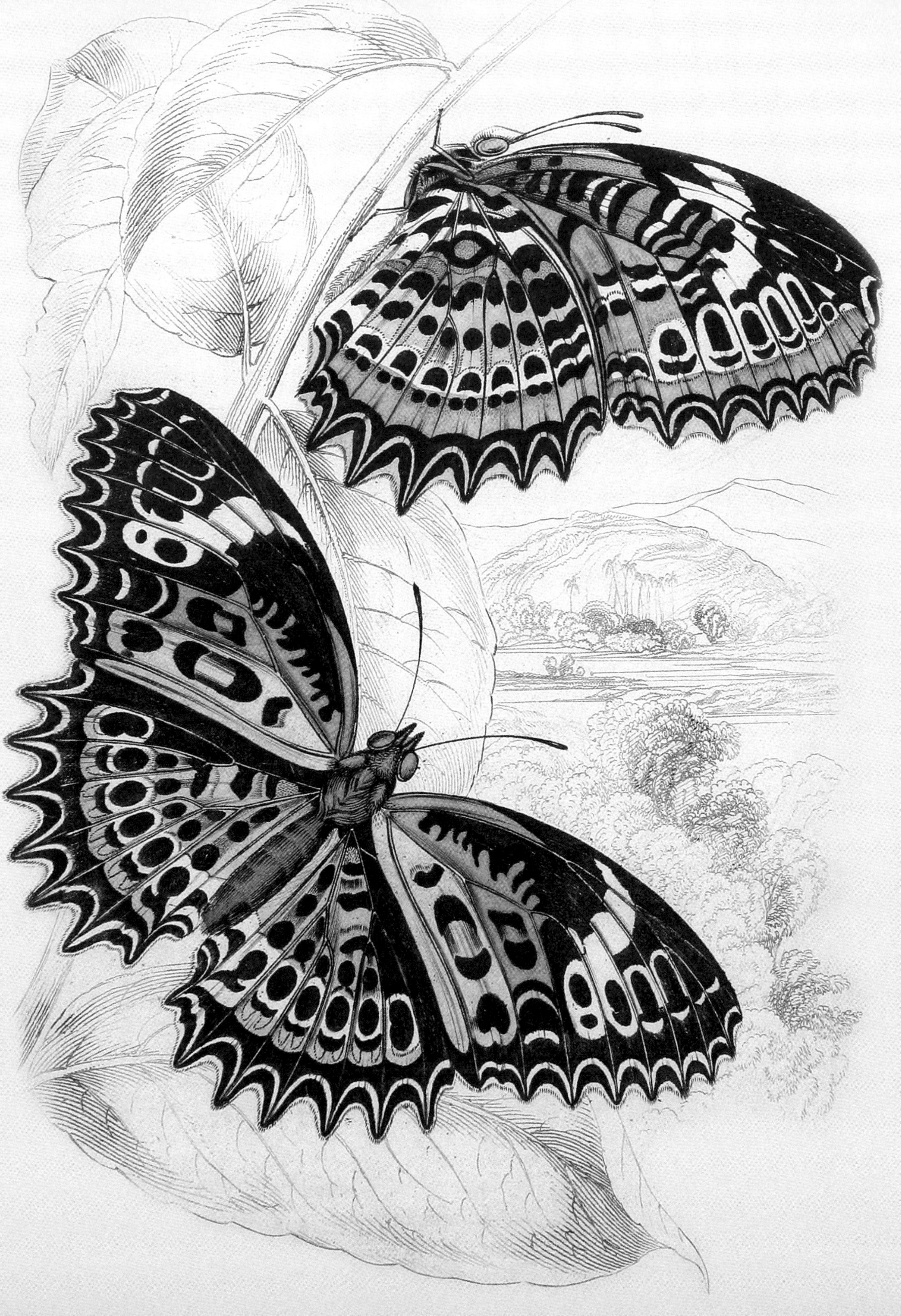

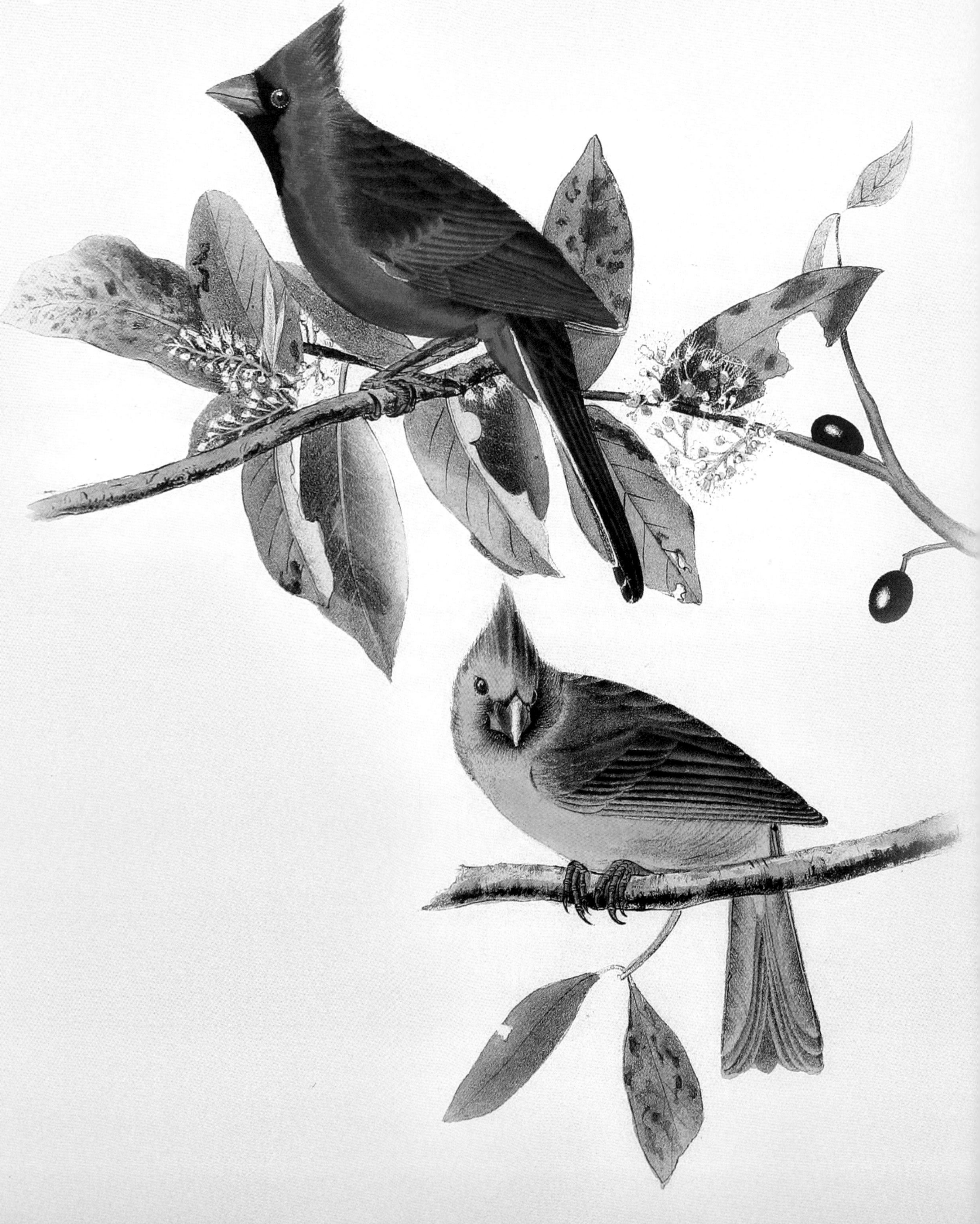

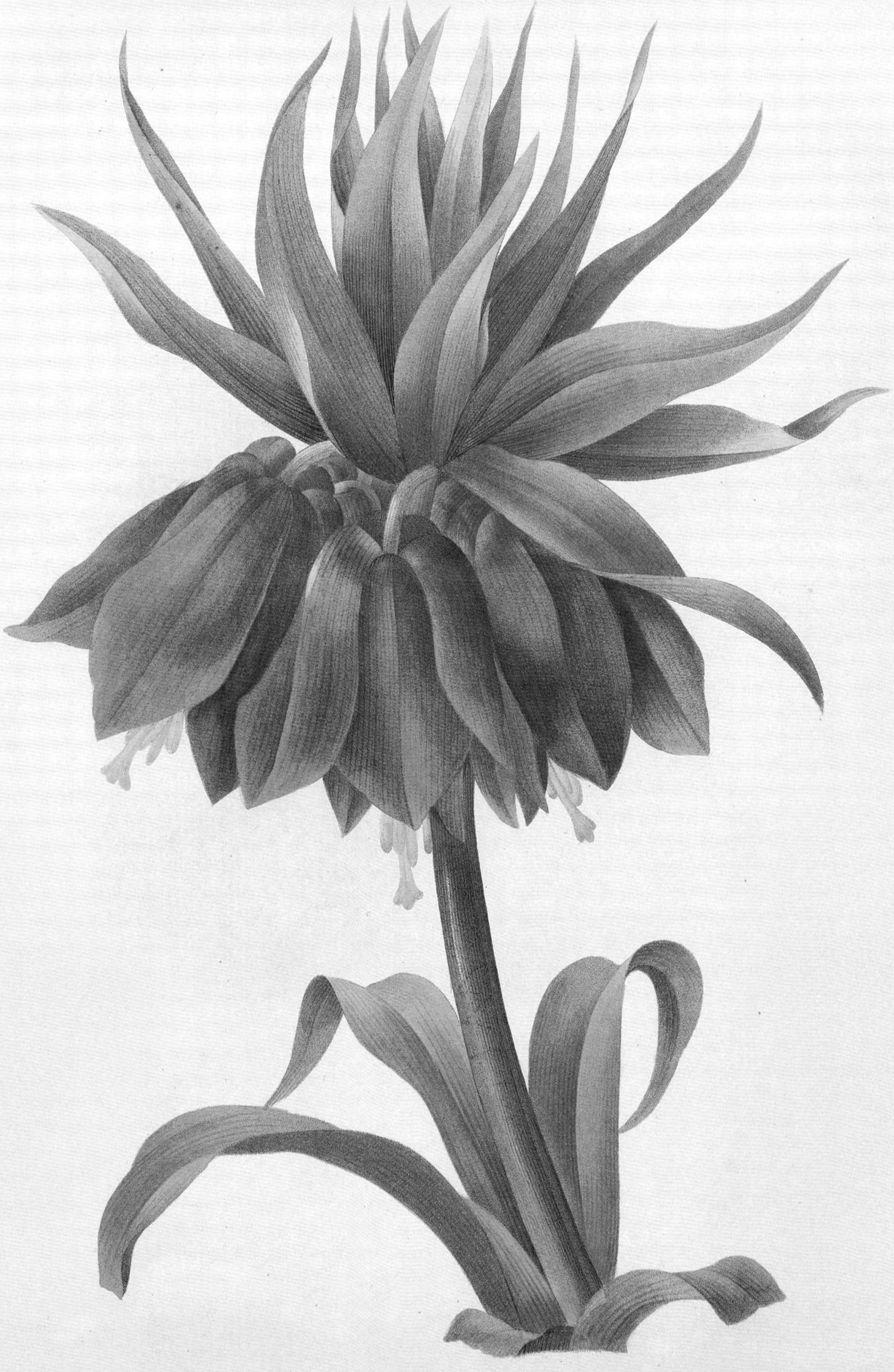

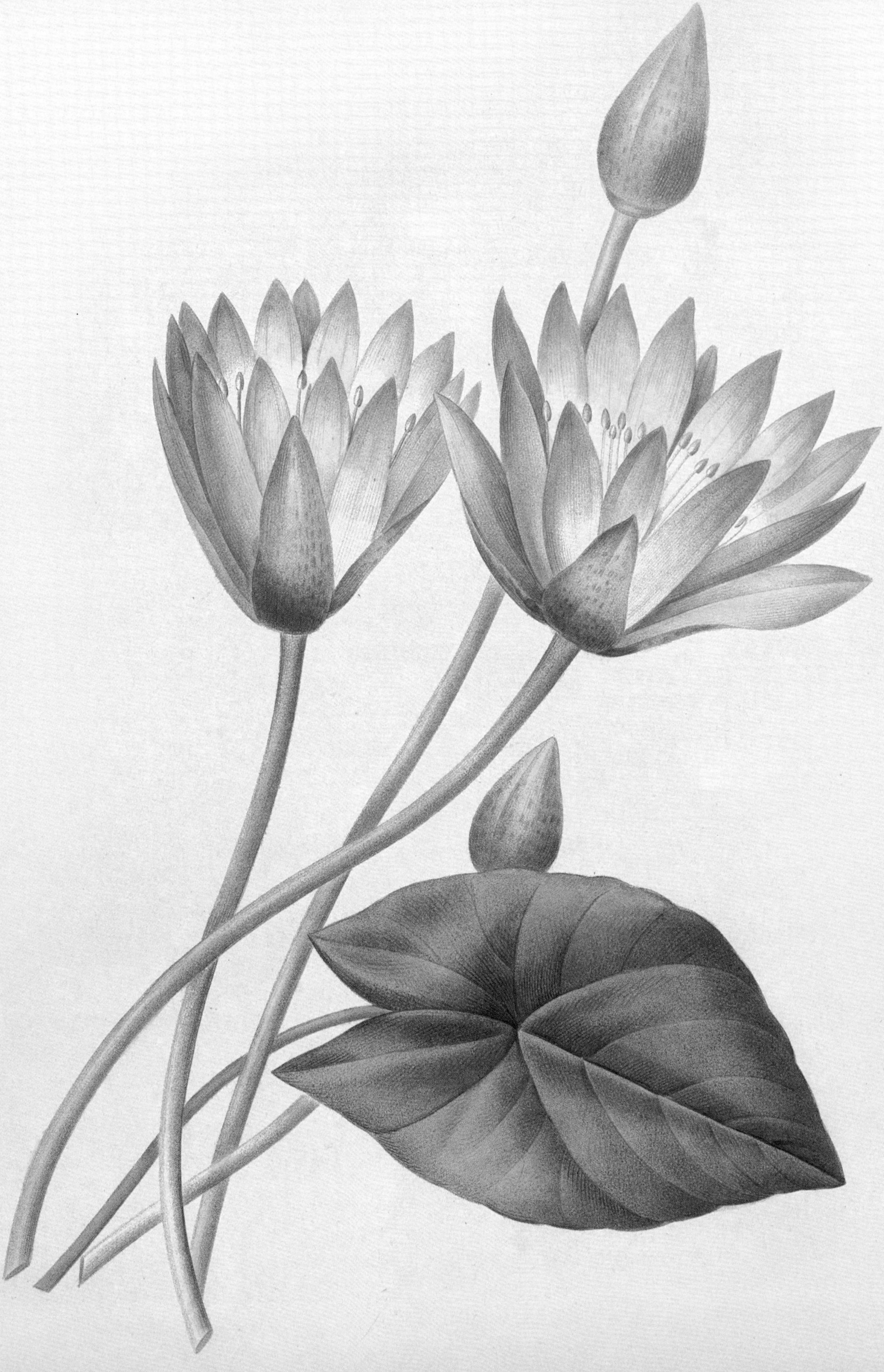

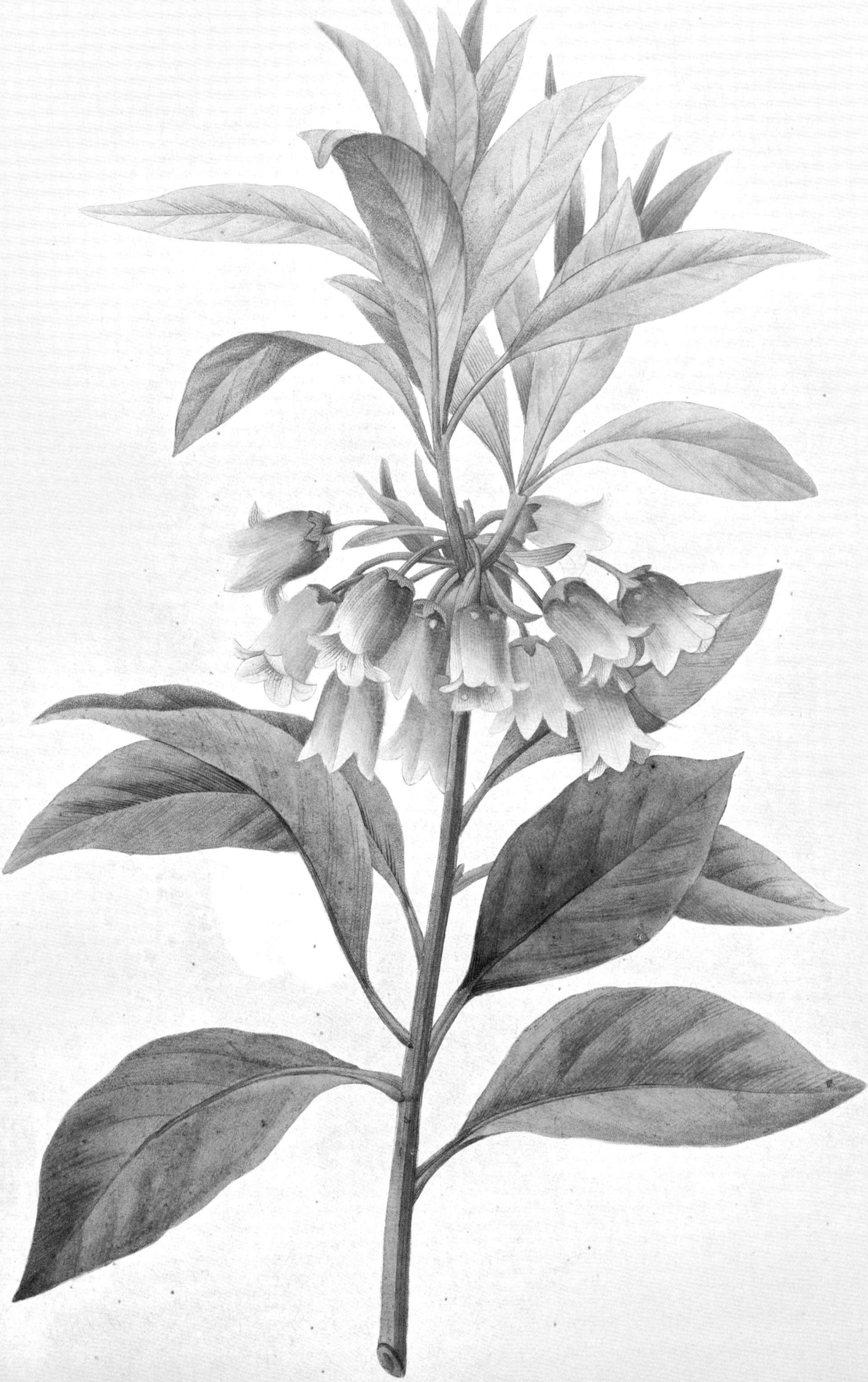

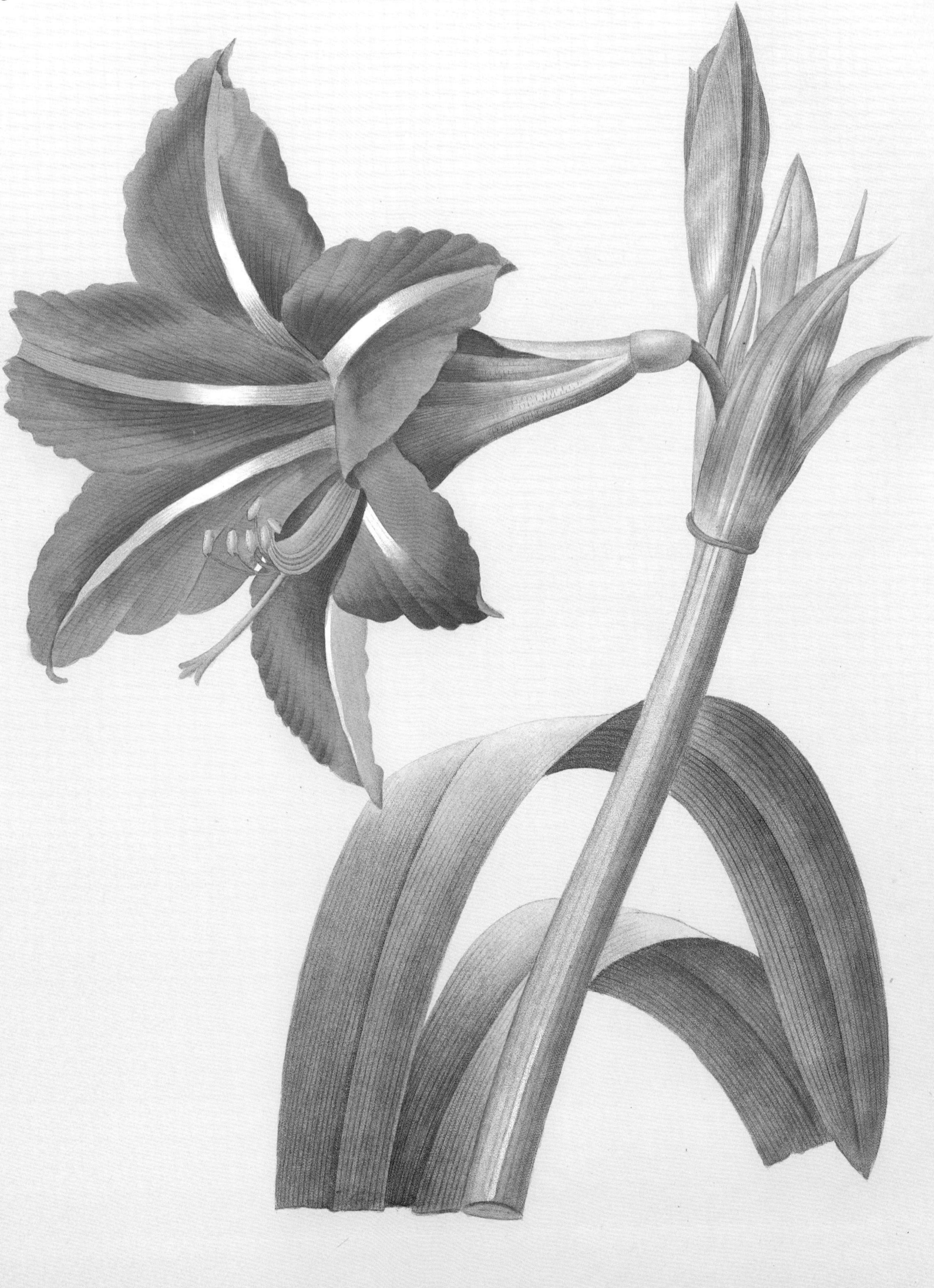

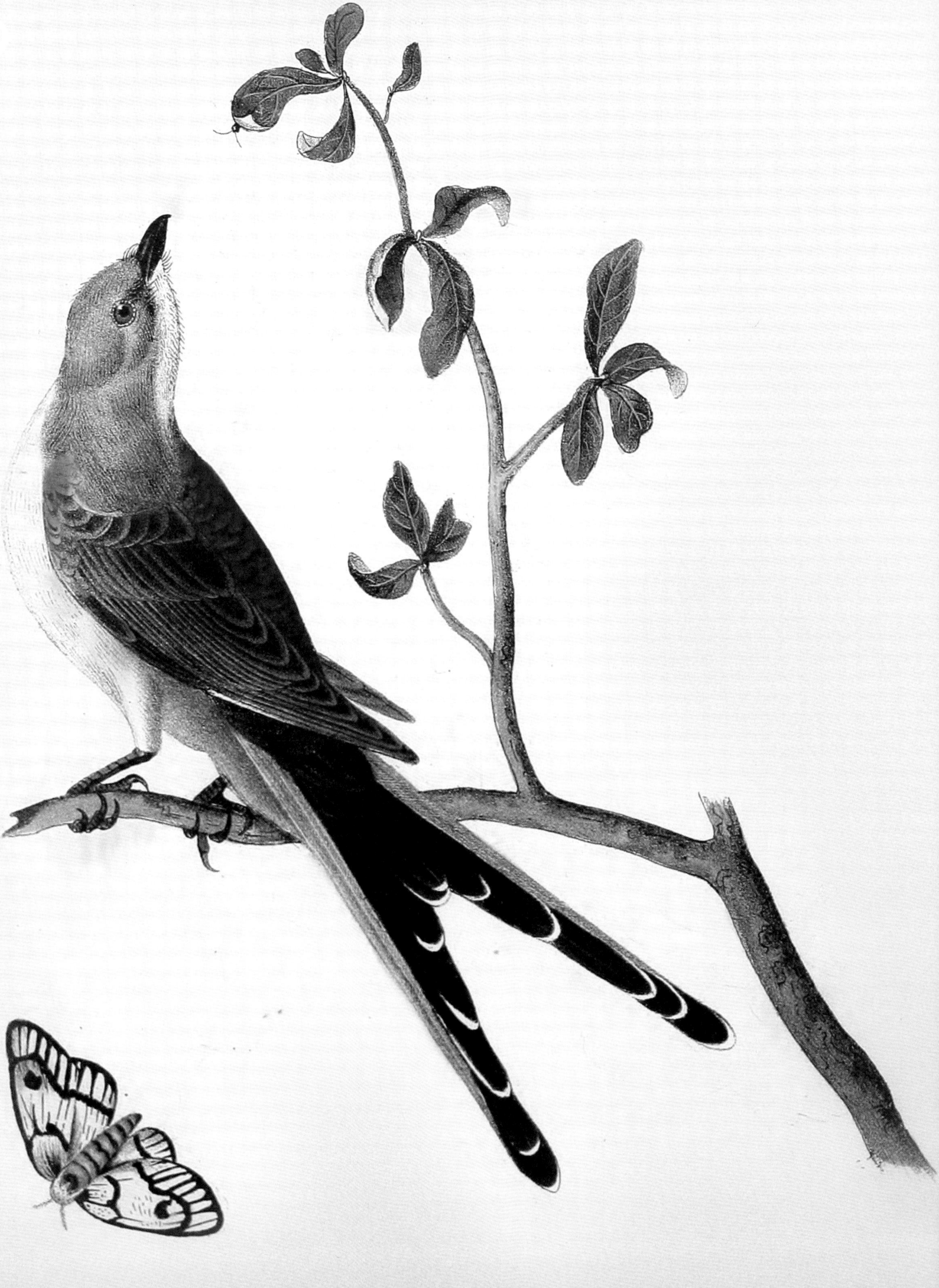

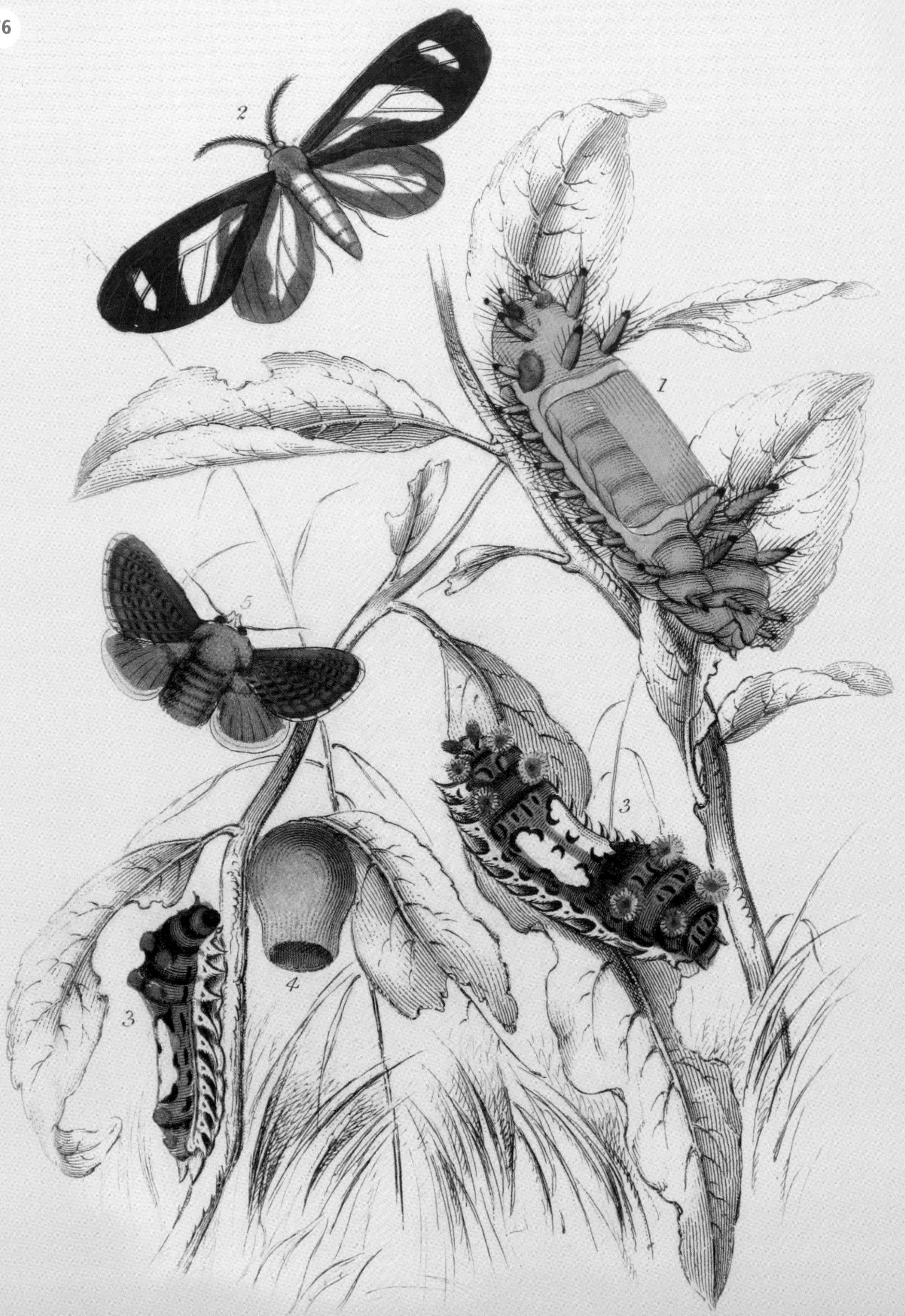
2
1
5
3
4
3

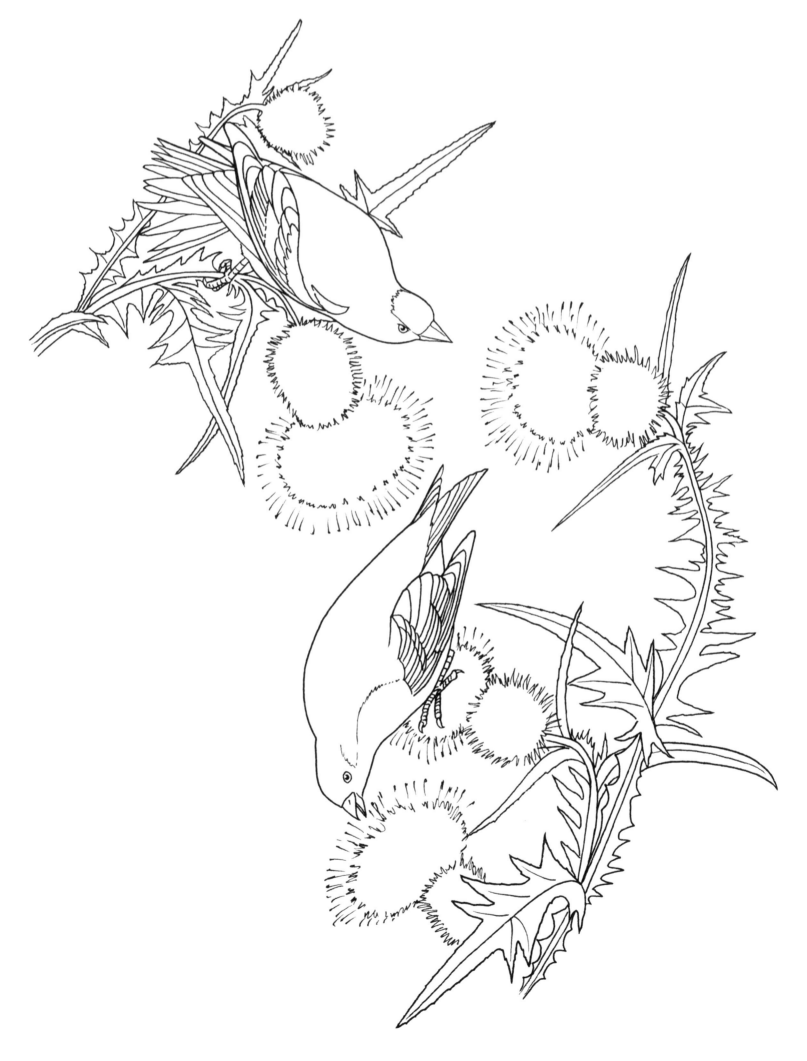

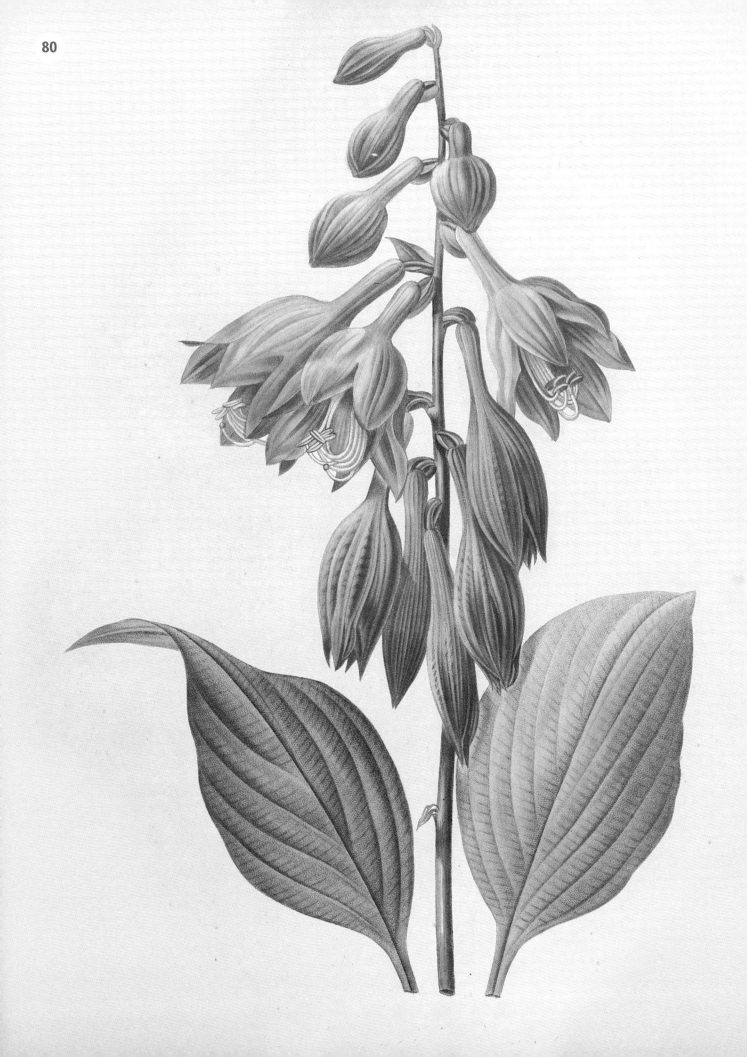

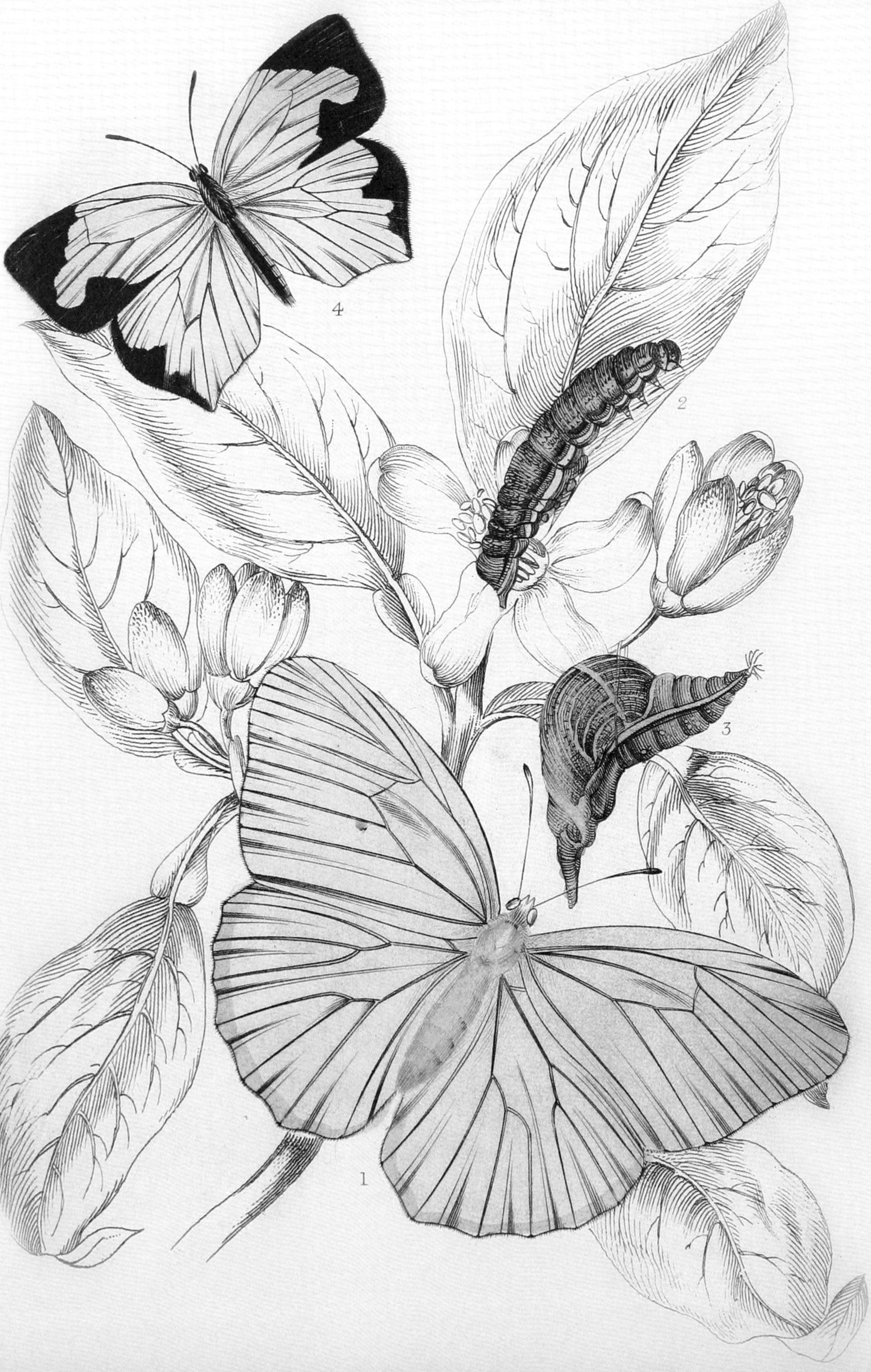
4
2
3
1

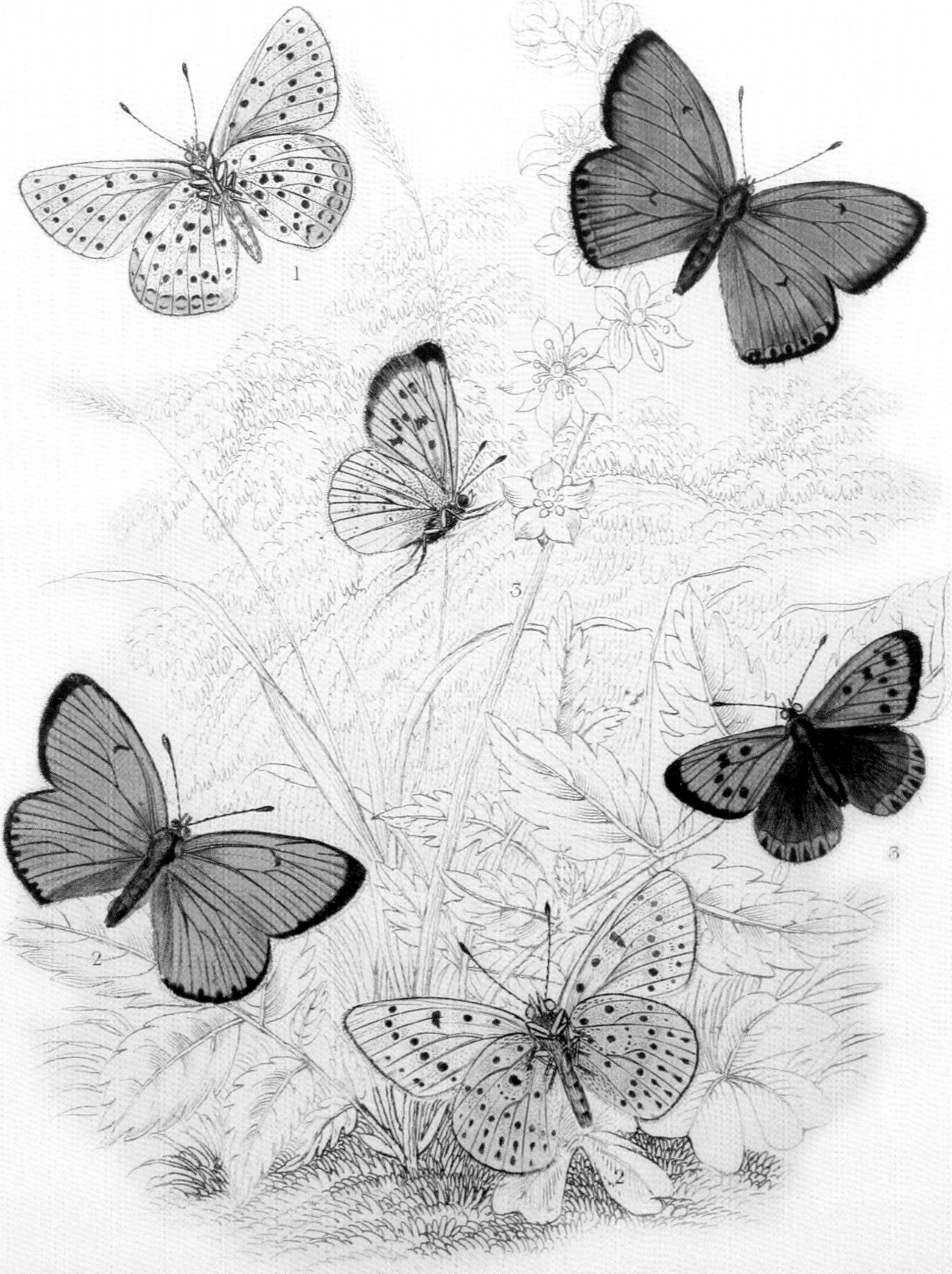
1
2
3
3
2
2

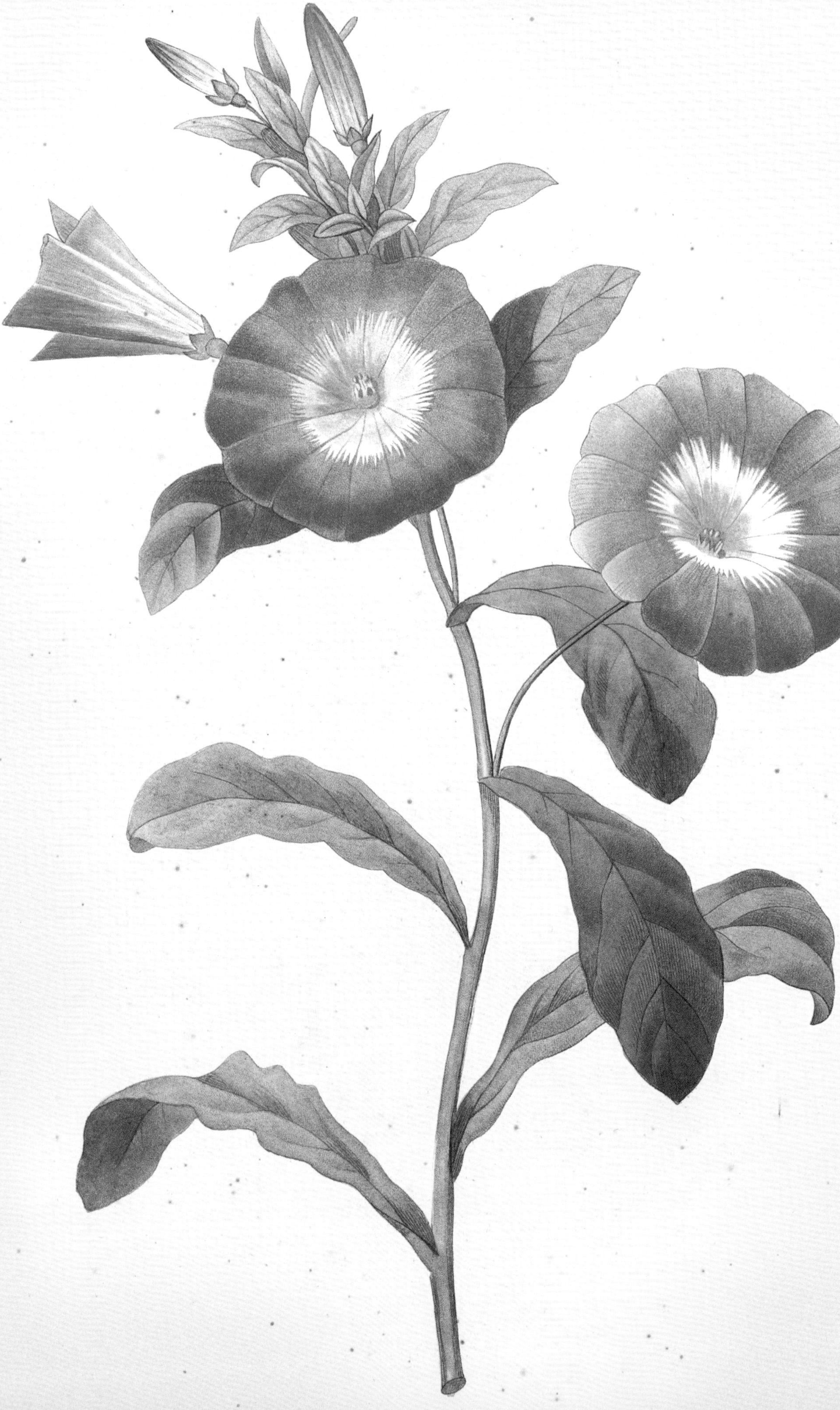

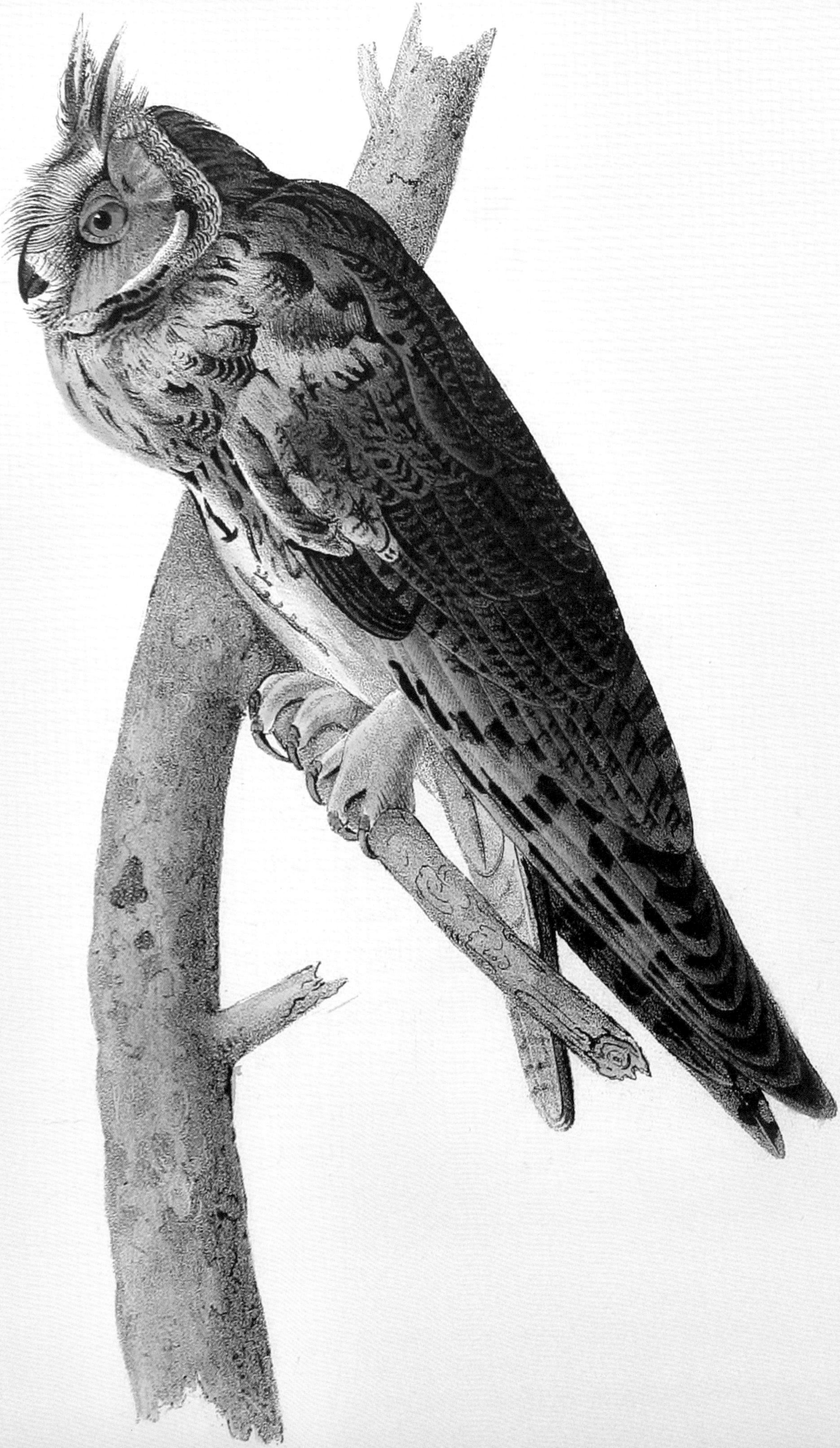

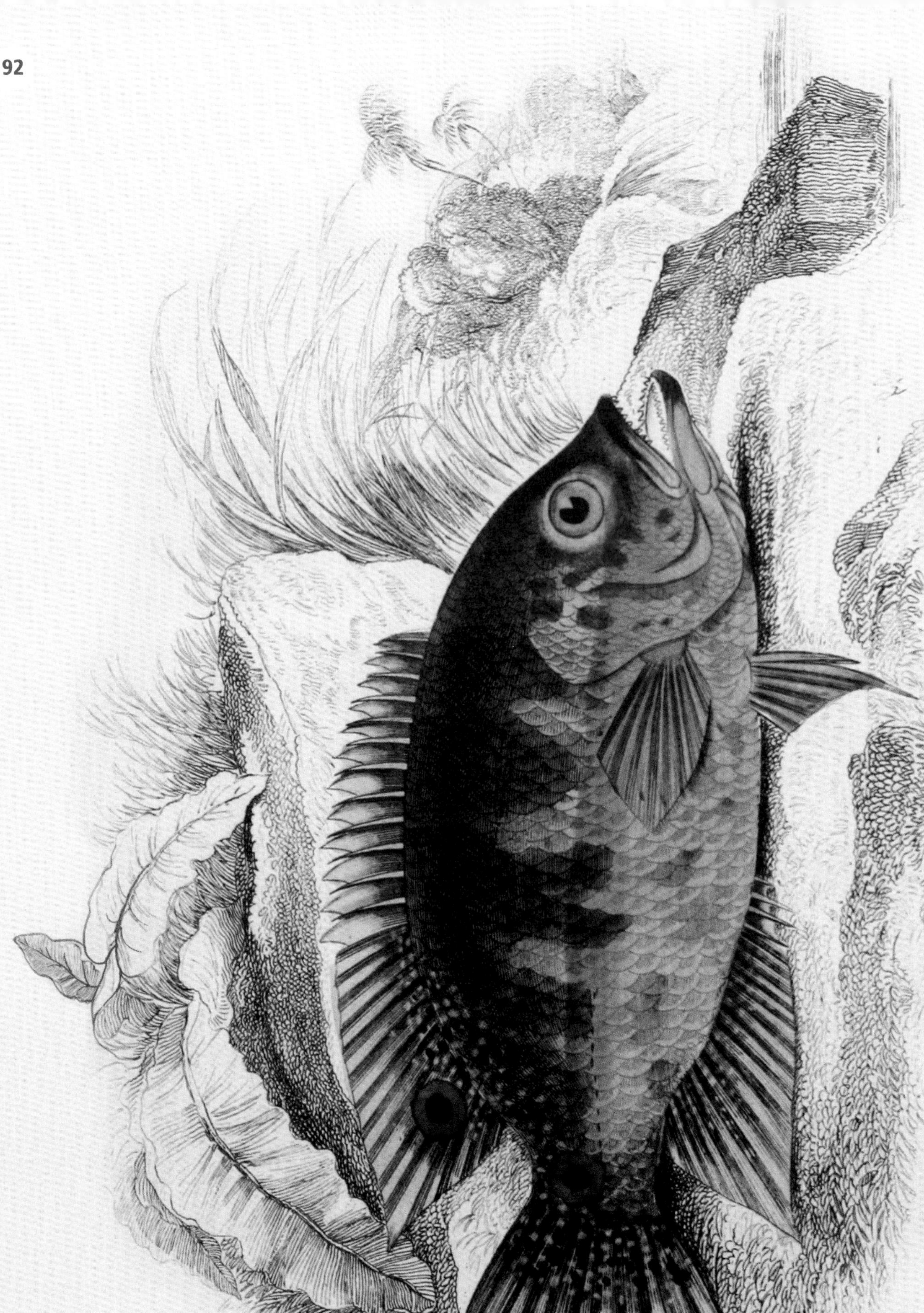

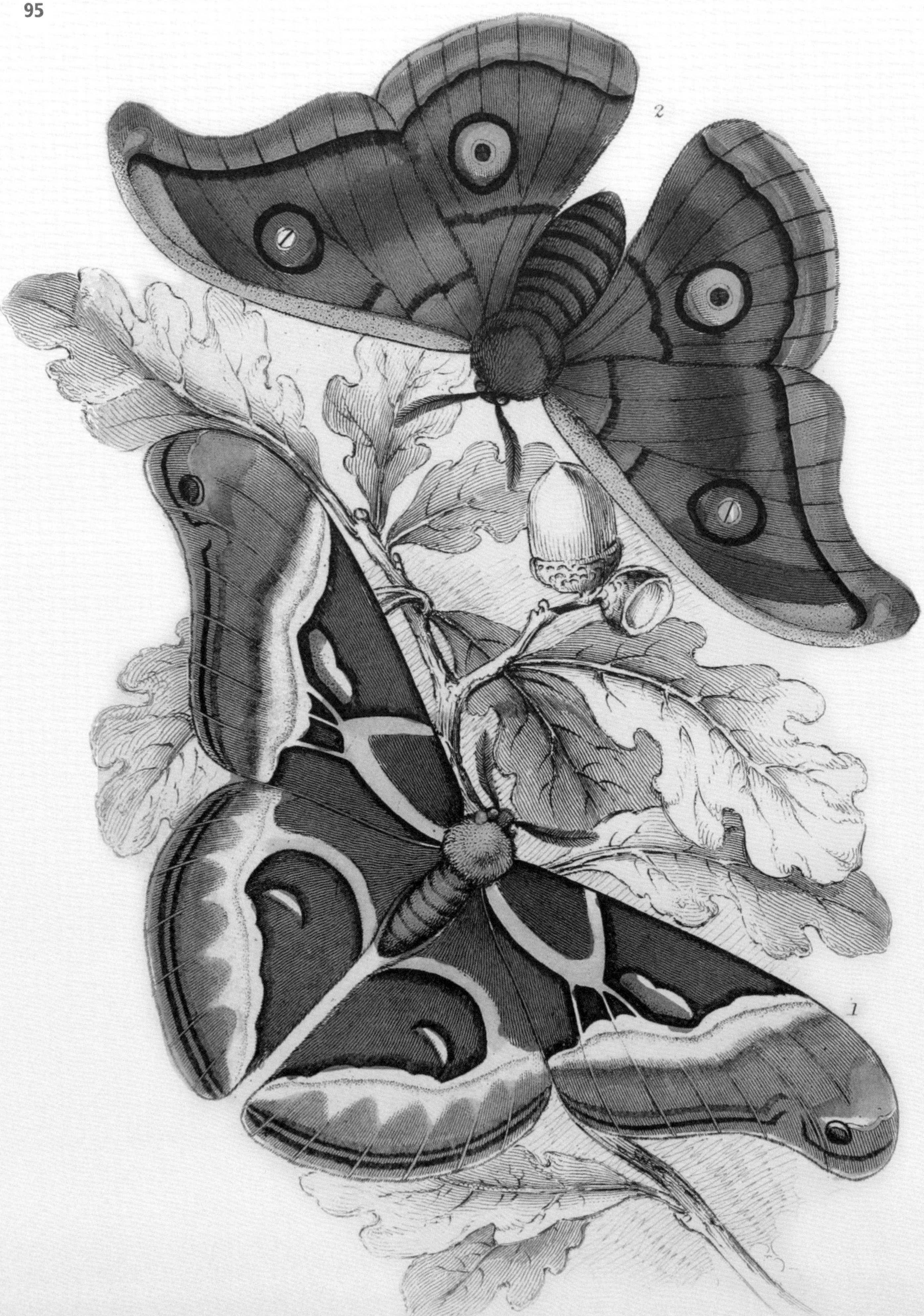
2
1

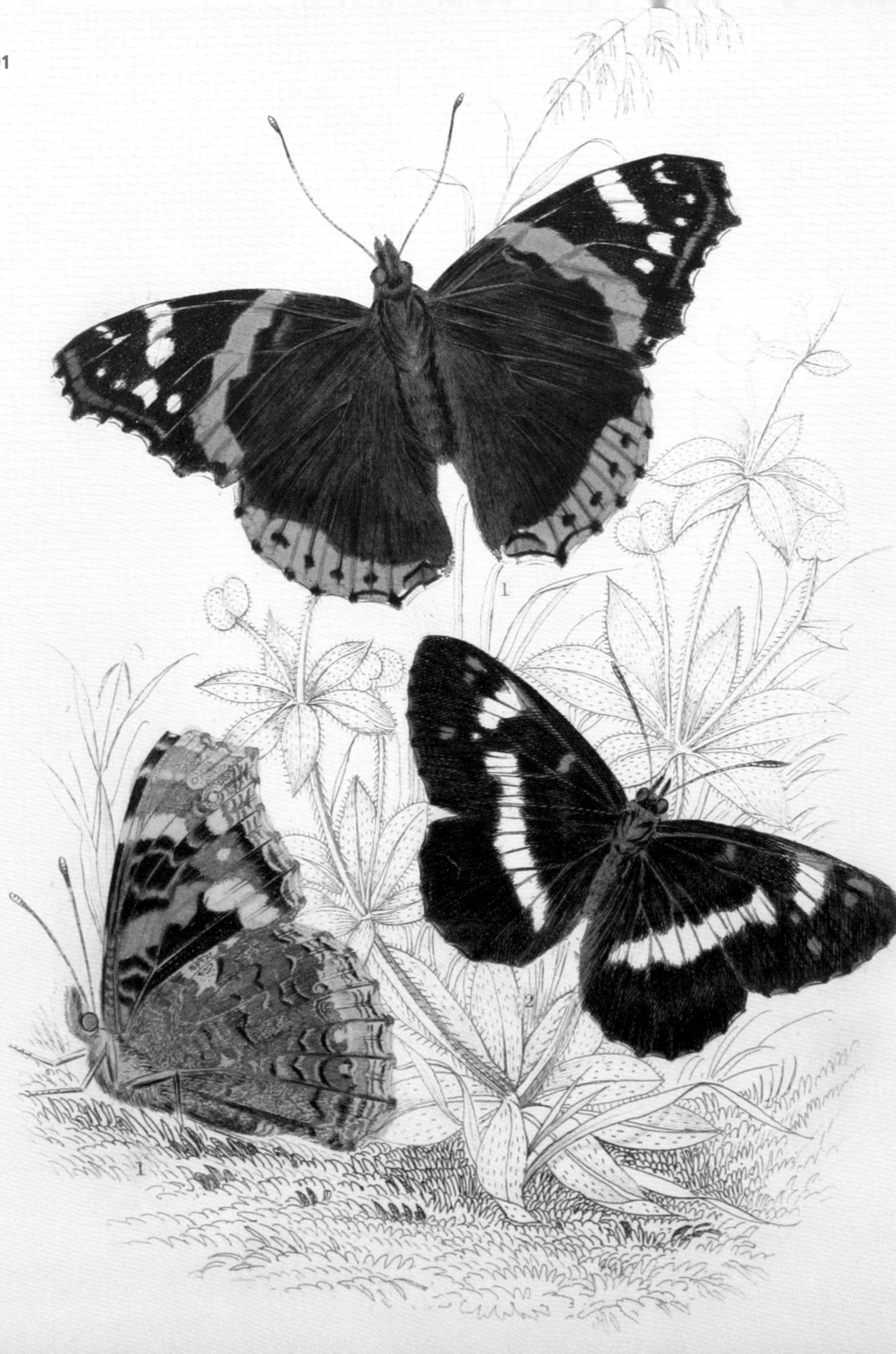
1
2
1

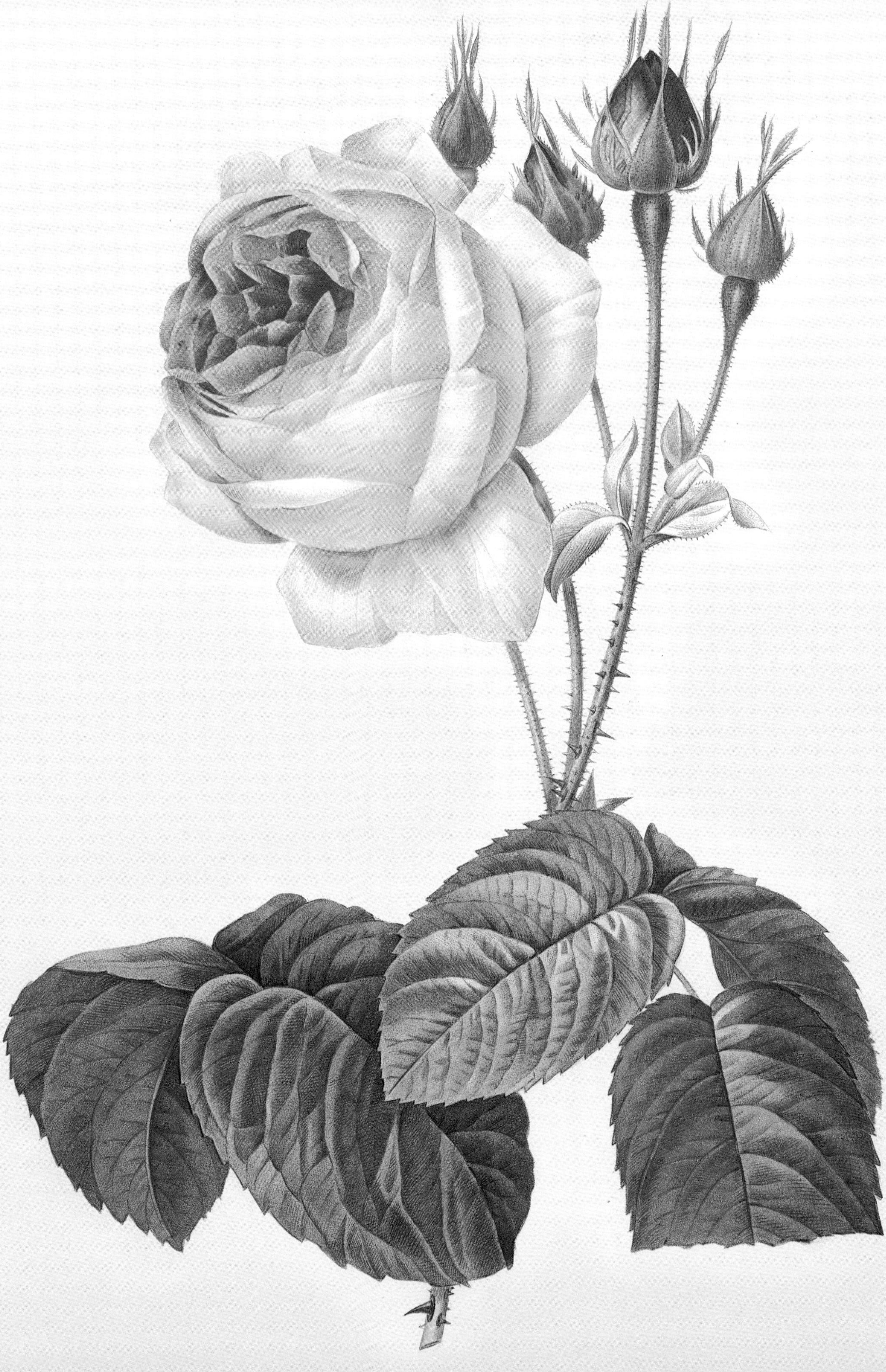

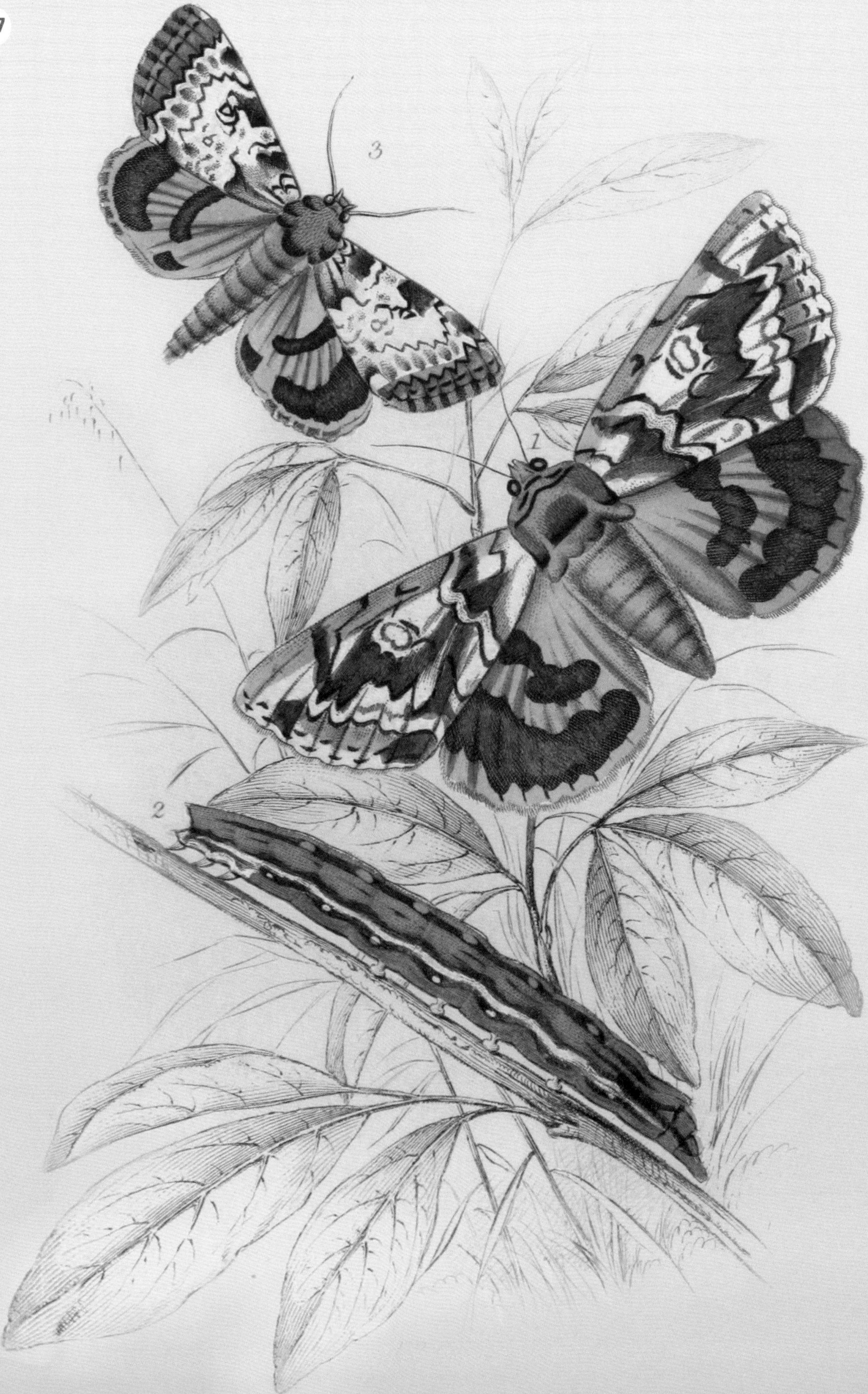
3
1
2

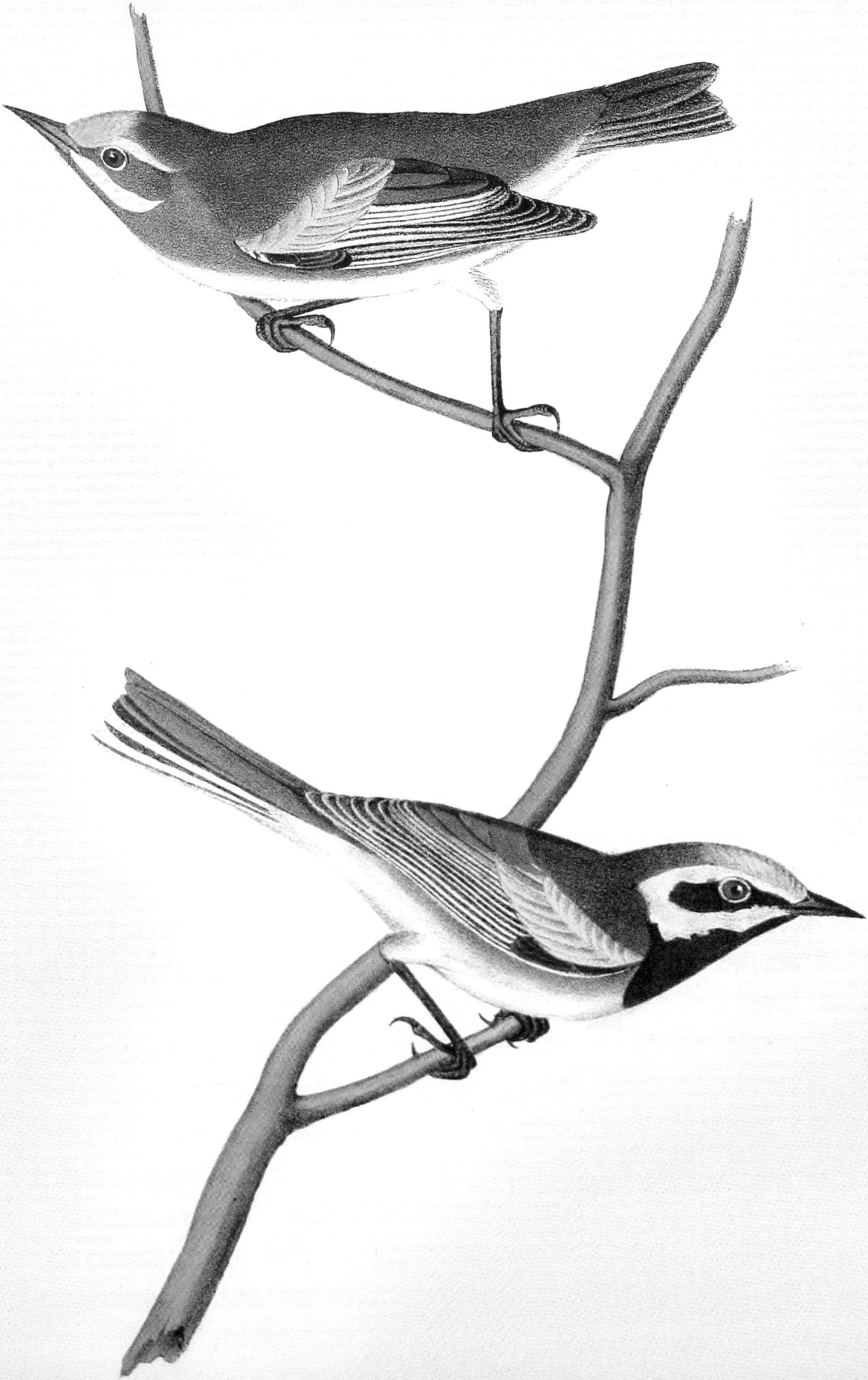

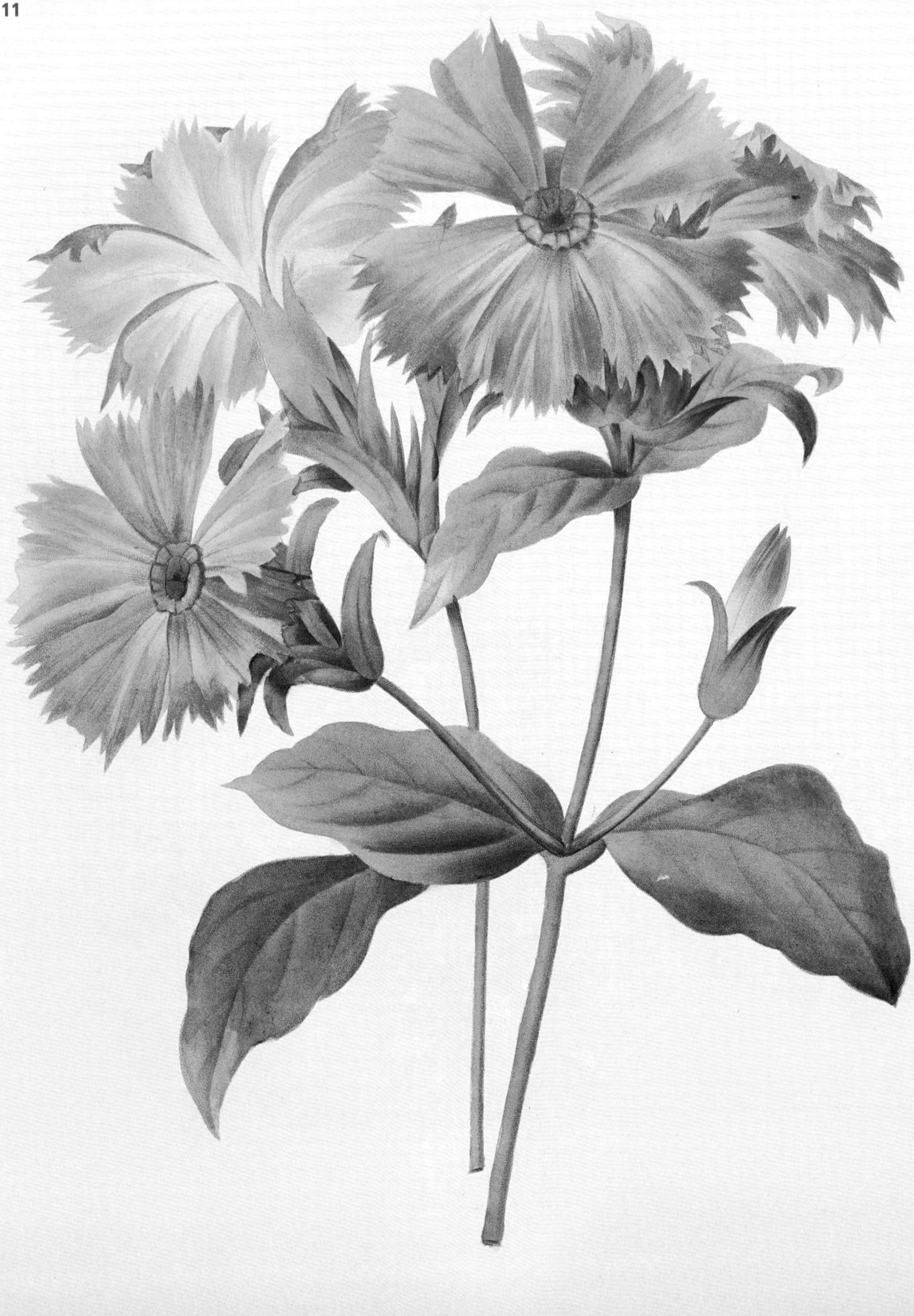

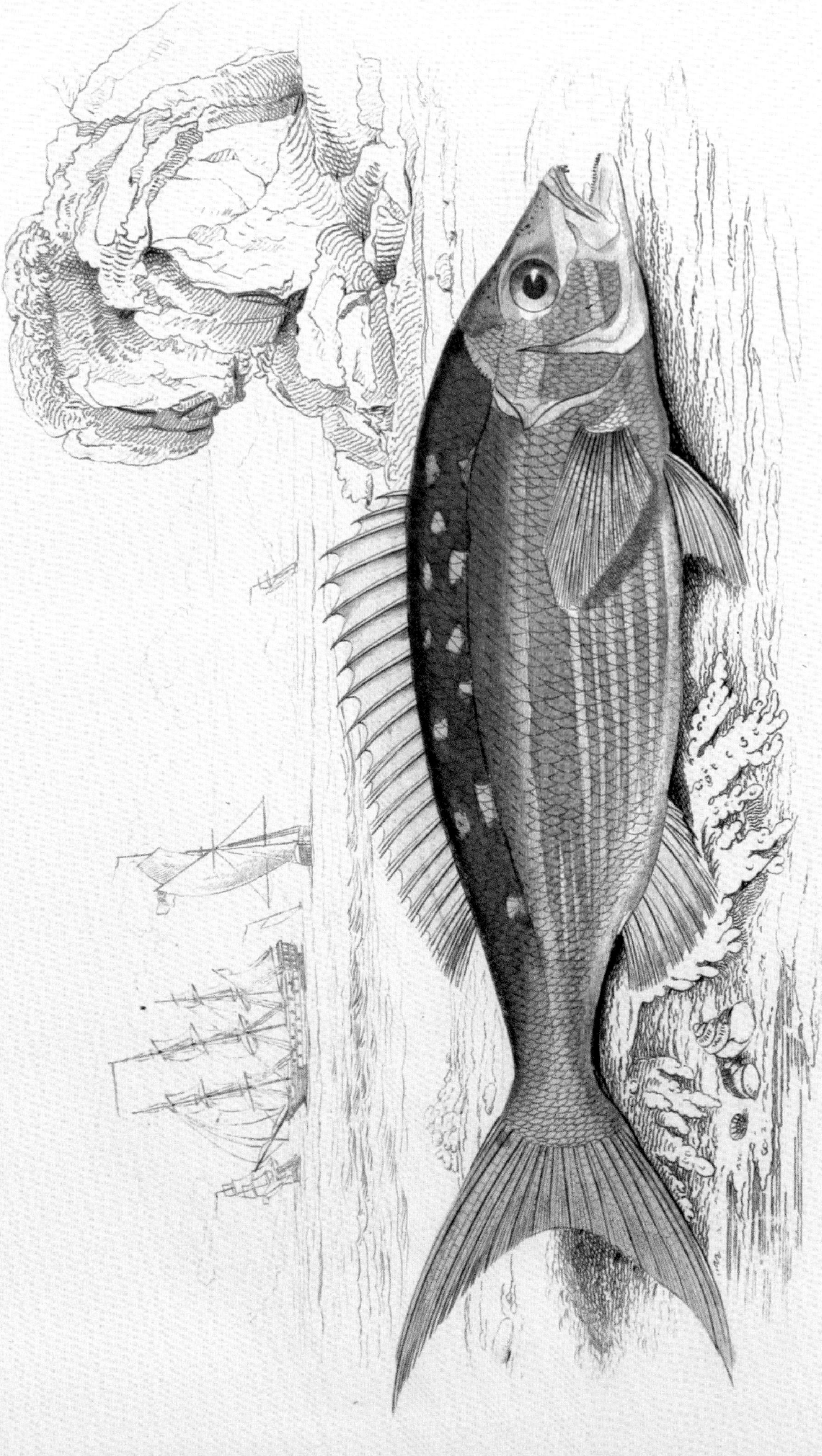

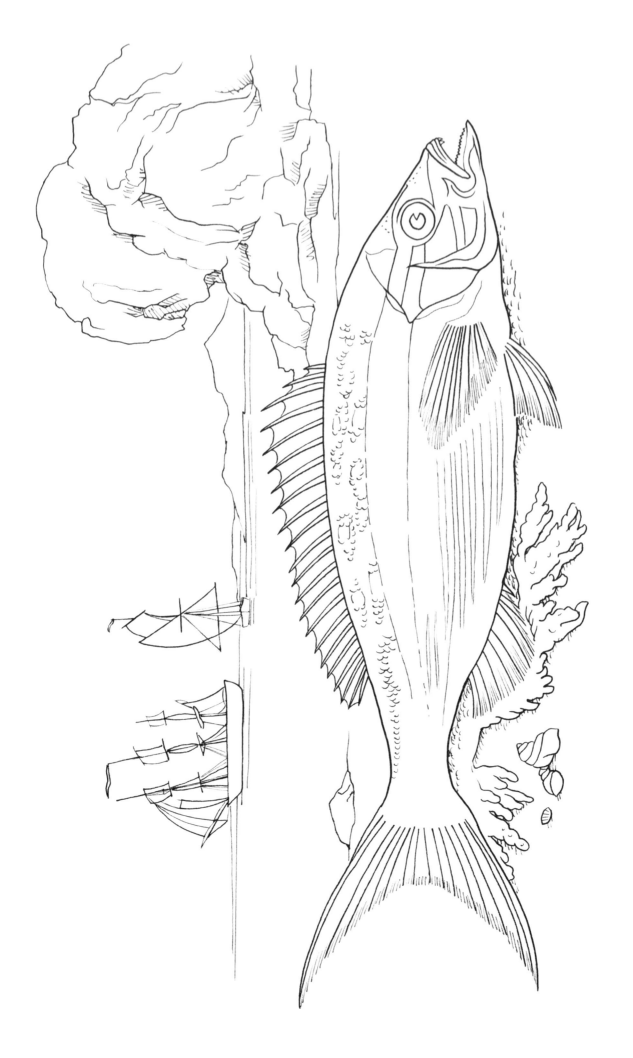

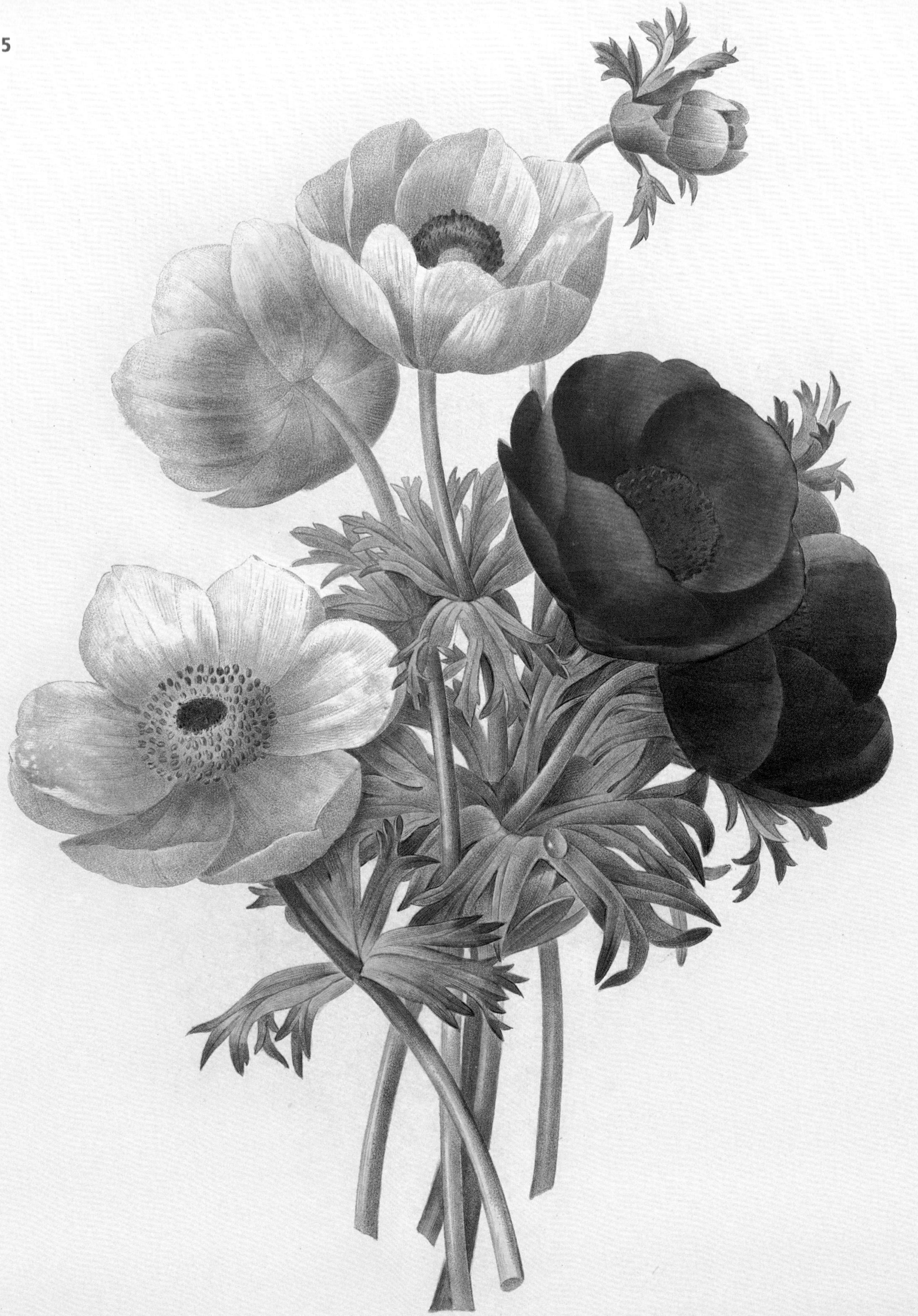

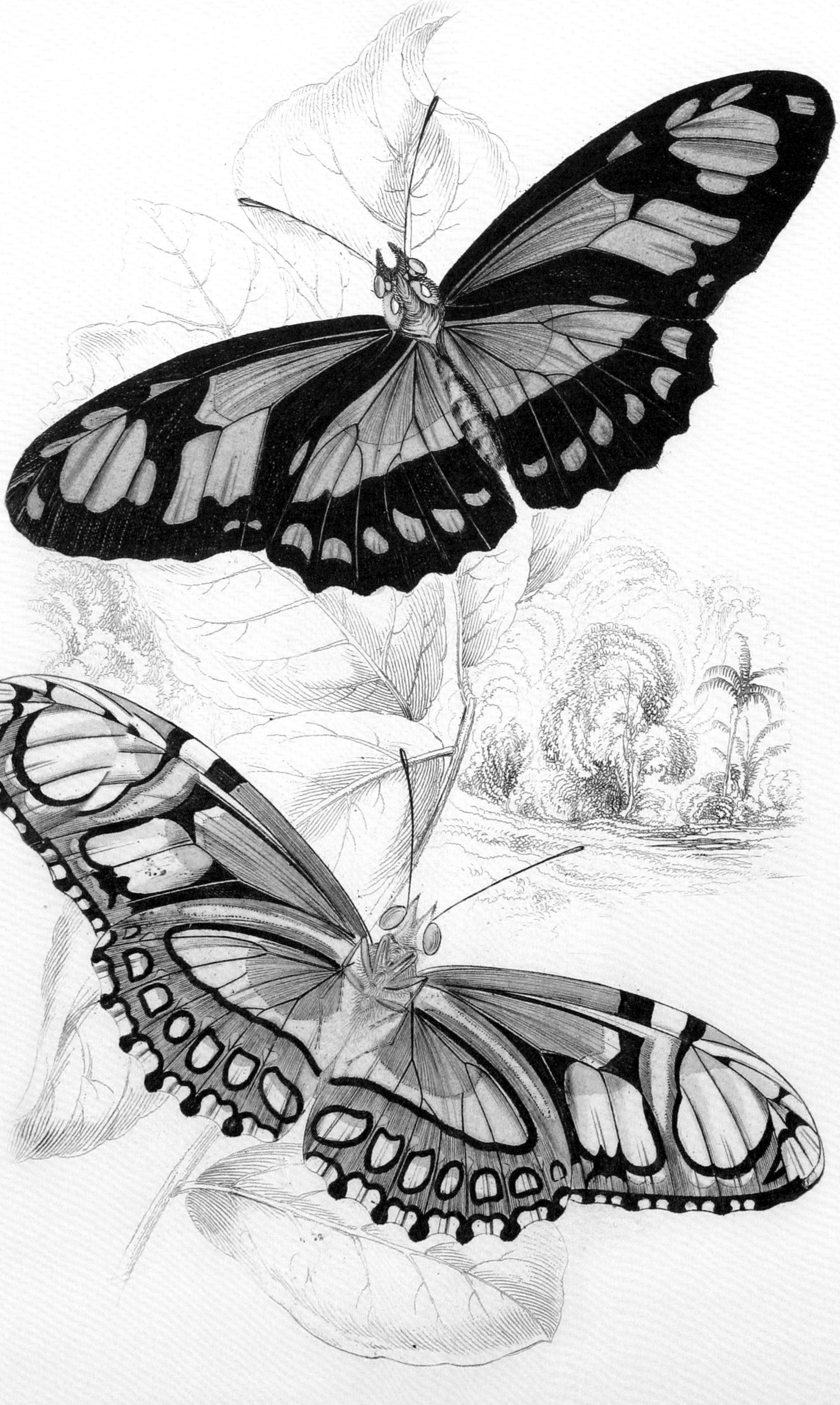

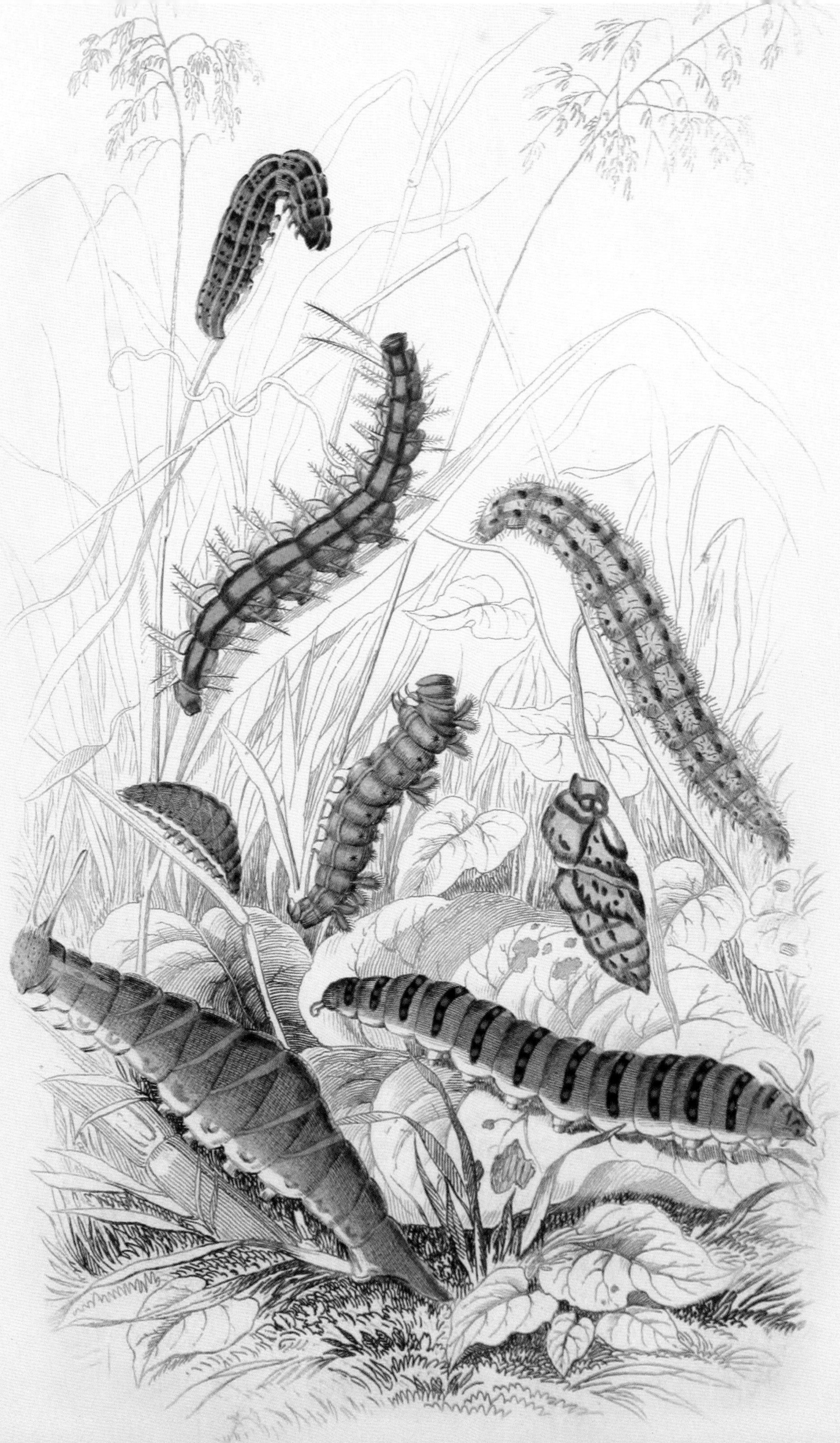